Career Skills for Young Adults Blueprint

A Step-by-Step Guide to Smarter Career Moves, Confident Salary Negotiation, and Sustainable Advancement Without Burnout or Guesswork

Noah Clark

Published by
Sprague Brook Publishing LLC

Paperback ISBN: 979-8-9947643-4-3

Printed in the United States of America

Legal Notice

The author and publisher make no representations or warranties regarding the accuracy or completeness of the information contained in this book. No responsibility or liability shall be assumed for any errors, omissions, or damages resulting from the use of this information.

Readers are responsible for their own actions, decisions, and results.

Disclaimer

This book is provided for educational and informational purposes only. It does not constitute legal, financial, medical, or professional advice. Although every effort has been made to ensure accuracy, no guarantees are made regarding outcomes or results.

Readers are encouraged to consult a qualified professional before applying any information contained in this book.

By reading this book, the reader acknowledges and agrees that the author and publisher shall not be held liable for any losses or damages, whether direct or indirect, arising from the use of this material.

Contents

Introduction

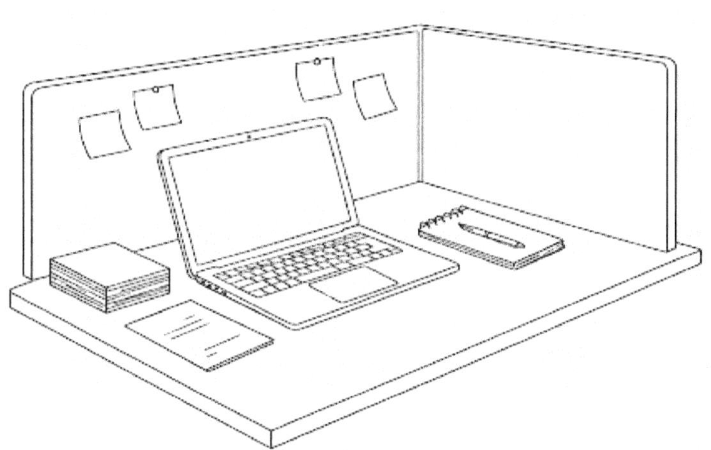

You're at your desk, blinking at your screen, trying to figure out whether you're making progress or just sprinting in place on a hamster wheel that costs too much. Meanwhile, your friends are out here talking about "growth opportunities" and "finding their calling," but all you've got is a to-do list that never shrinks and a paycheck that's been stuck in neutral for what feels like forever. Supposedly, you should be "networking," "negotiating," and "building your brand," but honestly, you have no idea what that even looks like in real life. Sometimes it feels like everyone else was handed a secret instruction manual, and you were out getting coffee when they passed it around.

If any of that sounds even a little bit like your life, pull up a chair. You're in good company. There's a reason so many of us end up feeling stuck, confused, or like we're just winging it at work. You don't need another vague pep talk that vanishes faster than your lunch break. You want actual steps, real tools, and a way forward that doesn't end with you burning out or turning into a human LinkedIn post.

Let's get specific about the problems we're here to tackle together:

- You're tired of hearing "just work harder" as the answer to every career question.
- You want to ask for a raise or promotion but dread that awkward, sweaty-palm conversation.
- You're ambitious, but you also value your sanity (and would like to keep your weekends for yourself).
- You crave actual direction, something better than a motivational quote taped to your monitor.
- You want to build momentum without guessing or gambling with your future.

Before we dive in, let's do a quick "Career Clarity Check." Grab a pen or just answer in your head. No judgment if you're reading this at your desk.

Career Clarity Check

1. Do you know exactly what skills you need to earn more in your current field?
2. Do you have a plan for making your work visible to the right people?
3. Are you confident in your ability to negotiate salary or promotions?
4. Do you feel clear on what you want next in your career?
5. Are you at risk of burnout, or do you feel like you're always "on"?
6. Do you ever second-guess your decisions, or worry you'll make the wrong move?
7. When you hear "network," do you picture something awkward and soul-draining?

If you nodded even internally to more than a couple of these, you're exactly who I wrote this book for.

So, why do I care so much about all this? Because I've watched way too many smart, hardworking people get stuck for years, just because nobody ever handed them a real-life blueprint for what to do next. I want to give you the tools I wish someone had given me, the ones that actually help real people, not just the ones with flawless résumés or superhero-level confidence.

Whom is this book for?

- You're early in your career, or you're making a switch.
- You want real progress, not just a fancier title.
- You want to negotiate without feeling like you're haggling at a flea market.
- You care about growth and stability, not hustle for hustle's sake.

- You're ready for frameworks, scripts, and checklists you can actually use.

Whom isn't this book for?

- You want a shortcut with no effort.
- You expect your boss to read your mind.
- You're looking for get-rich-quick schemes, generic motivation, or advice that works only if you're already a CEO.

What sets this book apart?

This isn't just another guide that tells you to "follow your passion" or "lean in." You'll find:

- Step-by-step frameworks to help you map your next move
- Ready-to-use scripts for real salary talks and tough conversations
- Case studies from people like you
- Checklists and exercises you can use as you go, not once, but whenever you need them.

You'll find quick prompts that encourage you to stop and think, along with exercises that fit into a real, busy life. I kept things practical, because, let's be honest: You do not have time for fluff.

When you look at what early-career professionals say frustrates them most, the same themes keep popping up in Amazon reviews and surveys:

- "Why does every career book assume I want to be a manager?"

- "Negotiation advice feels like it's written for extroverts in sales."
- "I want actionable steps, not another story about 'grit.'"

So, I built this whole blueprint around the real stuff people struggle with, using feedback from folks just like you.

Maybe you're thinking, *Okay, but will any of this actually work for me?* Maybe you've tried the one-size-fits-all advice, and it flopped. Maybe you're in tech, healthcare, nonprofits, or a job that never shows up in career books, and you're not sure this will fit. Or maybe you're just side-eyeing the idea of using a script with your boss. I get it. That's why you'll see examples from all kinds of jobs and people; every tip here has been tested in the wild.

Here's what you can expect by the end of this book:

- You'll have a clear path forward.
- You'll know how to make your achievements visible without feeling like a show-off.
- You'll have negotiation scripts that sound like you, not a robot.
- You'll build momentum that doesn't lead straight to burnout.
- You'll be able to spot opportunities, avoid dead ends, and keep moving, on your terms.

Let's keep it simple with a quick visual. Picture a pie with four equal slices, each representing a key part of sustainable career growth:

1. **Skills:** What you can do and how you keep learning
2. **Communication:** How you talk about your work and yourself

3. **Visibility:** Who knows about your results?
4. **Boundaries:** How you keep your work from eating your life

When all four work together, you don't just move forward; you roll forward, without the bumps and burnout.

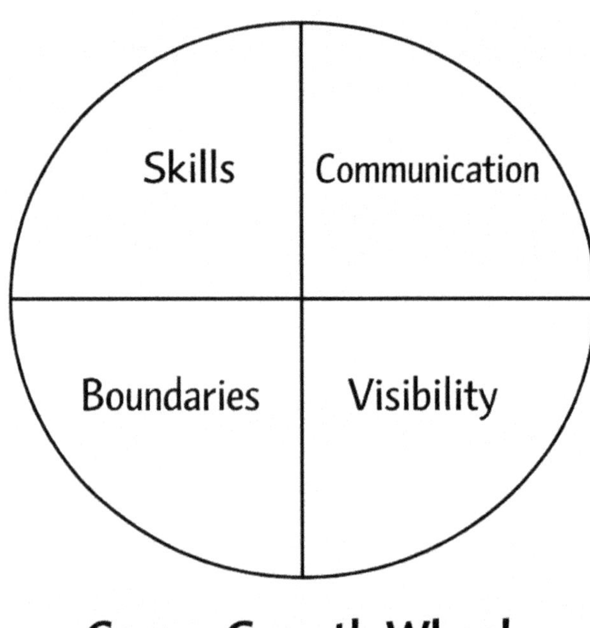

Career Growth Wheel

Here's how the book works: Each chapter tackles one piece of the puzzle: clarity, skill-building, visibility, negotiation, and sustainable momentum. Every chapter includes action steps, ready-to-use scripts, or checklists. You'll put strategies to work as you read, and you can come back to any section when you hit a new crossroad. This isn't a book you read once and shelve. It's a toolkit you'll use every time you make a move.

How to Use This Book

- Dive in and try the tools in real conversations and decisions.
- Reflect at the end of each chapter with the prompts.
- Revisit sections as your career evolves.
- Make notes, scribble in the margins, and keep this book close; your career won't stand still, and neither should your toolkit.

Now take a second and imagine what success would look like for you six months from now if you actually tried some of this stuff. More money? More confidence? More freedom? Maybe just a little less Sunday-night work anxiety?

You deserve a career that grows with you, not one that leaves you running on empty. Let's build that future together, one step at a time. Ready? Your blueprint's waiting.

Chapter 1

Foundations for Sustainable Career Growth

Have you ever been trapped at a family gathering and hit with the classic, "So, what are you doing now?" usually followed by a pep talk about "just working hard" or "sticking it out"? The urge to fake a bathroom emergency is real. Most career advice sounds like it was written when fax machines were the cutting edge. You want a job that actually lets you keep your weekends (and your sanity). This chapter is your chance to hit reset. We'll bust some outdated myths, get honest about what helps you move up these days, and set you up for real, sustainable success. No sugarcoating. Just the good stuff, with a few laughs along the way.

Busting Career Myths: What Drives Advancement Today

Time to drag some of the biggest career myths into the light. First up: "Hard work always gets noticed." Wouldn't that be nice? In reality, working your tail off in silence is like whispering into a hurricane: No one hears you. You could be crushing it, but if you never speak up or let anyone see your wins, it's like you're wearing an invisibility cloak.

The people who move up are the ones who aren't afraid to show their impact, build connections, and, yes, sometimes talk about themselves, even if it makes them cringe a little.

Then there's the old chestnut: "Stay loyal and you'll be rewarded." Maybe you grew up hearing that patience is a virtue, but these days, waiting quietly in the corner is more likely to get you a permanent seat there. Job-hopping isn't just normal now; it's often how people level up, learn new things, and find a better fit. Sitting tight and hoping someone notices you usually leads to feeling stuck, not promoted.

And let's not forget: "Technical skills alone are enough." Sure, you've heard about the coding wizard or design genius who gets showered with praise. But here's the plot twist: It's usually the people who can effectively talk to other humans, adapt on the fly, and work well with a team who get ahead. If you're an analyst who can't explain your findings, or a developer who treats teamwork like a group project from high school, you'll probably get passed over for someone who's got better people skills in their toolkit.

Career Myths Reality Check

- Believing hard work will speak for itself
- Thinking loyalty guarantees promotion
- Assuming technical skills outweigh soft skills
- Waiting to be noticed instead of self-advocating
- Steering clear of networking because it feels awkward

If you're nodding along to any of these, don't worry. You're not broken. These are just old-school ideas that might be tripping you up.

Myths vs. Reality

Myths	Reality
Hard work speaks for itself	Visibility and networking matter
Loyalty guarantees promotion	Adaptability leads to growth
Just focus on technical skills	Soft skills are essential too

So, what helps you move up these days? First, you've got to build new skills. Think volunteering for projects that scare you a little, or learning things that match where your field is going, not just where it's been. Second, ask for feedback like it's free pizza. Don't wait for the annual review; check in often and treat every bit of input as a mini–coaching session. Third, get used to talking about your wins. It's not bragging; it's just being honest. Try mentioning your contributions in meetings or one-on-ones, even if it makes you want to hide under the table at first.

Consider these real-life stories: Sam, a remote developer, started sharing weekly Slack updates, not just code, but wins and insights. Leadership began to see his impact and soon offered him a stretch project. Priya, working at a nonprofit with few promotions, built new skills by taking online courses and told her manager how she could use them to help her team. She wasn't just promoted; she landed a role tailored to her strengths. Or Jordan, a first-gen healthcare professional, who felt unnoticed at meetings until he started preparing questions and sharing insights. Colleagues, and then his boss, started seeking him out.

Even if you're more introvert than spotlight-stealer, or your company hands out fancy titles like rare Pokémon cards, these strategies still work. You can advocate for yourself with a quick email update or a one-on-one chat. Moving up doesn't always mean chasing a manager title; it could be a sideways move, owning a cool project, learning a new skill, or carving out your own weirdly perfect niche.

Reflection prompt: Which career myth have you believed the longest? How has it affected your approach to visibility or advancement? Write down one old belief you're ready to challenge, then consider what might be possible if you let it go.

Clarifying Your Career Compass: Values, Strengths, and Non-Negotiables

Figuring out what you want from your career isn't as simple as picking a job title and hoping for the best. You probably already know that, but it's way too easy to slip into autopilot and chase what everyone else seems to be chasing. Most of us are handed a list of "success" milestones by society: Get promoted, earn more, climb higher, and go after them like there's only one finish line. But here's the thing: Your definition of "success" might look nothing like your roommate's, your sibling's, or your boss's. Maybe you crave autonomy, or you want to make an impact, or you just want stability so you can enjoy your evenings. You might value creativity or crave a sense of belonging at work. The trick is getting brutally honest about what lights you up and what drains you. So, grab a pen or your phone and jot down what really matters: Is it flexibility? Learning new things? Financial security? Room for side projects?

Here's a quick self-assessment to spark ideas:

- Which moments at work give you energy instead of sucking it away?
- What are three things you absolutely need in a job?
- When did you last feel proud of something you accomplished?
- What would make you quit, even if your salary were doubled?

Now, let's dig into strengths because knowing what you're good at is just as important as knowing what you value. Maybe you're the go-to person for troubleshooting tech issues, or perhaps people come to you for advice because you listen without judging. Sometimes strengths hide in plain sight because they come so naturally that you don't even notice them. If you want some science behind this, check out Clifton-Strengths or VIA Character Strengths (they're like BuzzFeed quizzes but actually useful for your career). Or try the Myers-Briggs Type Indicator if you're curious about how your personality shapes your work style. Don't stop there; look through old performance reviews, emails from happy clients, or even texts from coworkers who thanked you for saving the day. Map these wins and feedback into a strengths inventory. Write down three things people often compliment you on (even if it feels awkward). Your unique combo of skills and quirks is more valuable than you think.

Boundaries and red lines matter just as much. It's tempting to say yes to everything when you're new or eager to grow, but that's how burnout sneaks in. Think about the stuff you absolutely won't compromise on. Maybe it's remote work, maybe it's a boss who respects time off, or a company that values diversity over lip service. Sketch out your non-negotiables: Is it working no more than 40 hours a week? Refusing to take calls after dinner? Refusing to work for a company whose mission doesn't align with yours? These boundaries protect your well-being and keep resentment from taking root.

Career Compass Snapshot Checklist

My top three values: ____

My core strengths: ____

My non-negotiables: ____

Keep this list somewhere you'll see it. Trust me, you'll want it when you're weighing a new job, prepping for an interview, or just wondering if it's time to make a run for it.

Time for a little reflection: When did you last feel truly excited at work, not just caffeinated, but genuinely energized? What were you doing, who was around, and why did it feel good? Paint a picture of your best "good day" on the job. Now, flip it: What would make you bolt, even if the paycheck was huge? These aren't just journal prompts; they're your secret weapon for making better choices.

One last gut check: Does your job, your boss, or even your team vibe match what matters to you? Or are you constantly making excuses and telling yourself, *Eh, it's fine, I guess?* Take two minutes to jot down one thing that lines up with your values and one thing that's way off. This is your personal compass; use it to dodge the energy vampires and find the places where you'll thrive.

Building Your Career Map: Choosing Paths Beyond the Corporate Ladder

Imagine looking at a map, but instead of neat highways, it's all squiggles, shortcuts, and a few paths that double back just for fun. That's what careers look like now, definitely not a straight climb to the corner office. The old-school "one promotion after another" ladder is just one way up. These days, it's more like a jungle gym, and your path can go up, sideways, diagonally, or off into the wild blue yonder (cue your high school guidance counselor sweating). Picture three options: the classic straight-up arrow (ladder), a zigzagging path (lattice), and a web of roles all connected (portfolio). That last one's for the rebels and creative types who want to mix things up, like juggling freelance gigs, part-time work, or consulting on the side. Portfolio careers are catching on, especially if you want flexibility, variety, or a backup plan when the world gets weird.

Career Paths

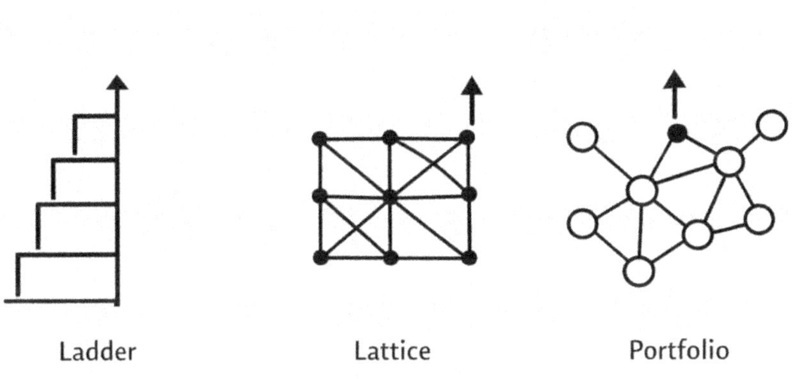

If your brain is spinning with options and you're stuck in analysis paralysis, try the good old **SWOT** analysis. Grab a blank page and split it into four boxes: **Strengths, Weaknesses, Opportunities, Threats**. Say you're thinking about jumping from finance to UX design. Jot down your strengths (maybe you're detail-obsessed), weaknesses (no design portfolio yet), opportunities (UX jobs are booming), and threats (hello, steep learning curve). This trick works whether you're choosing between two job offers or daydreaming about teaching English in another country. It forces you to get real about what's awesome and what might trip you up.

But don't just fall down the rabbit hole of Googling job descriptions or doom-scrolling LinkedIn. The real magic? Talking to people who are already doing the thing you're curious about. Set up a quick chat, ask what their day looks like, what's tough, and what they wish they'd known before jumping in. Not sure what to say? Try this: "Hi

[Name], I'm curious about [role/industry] and would love 15 minutes to hear about your experience. Totally get it if you're swamped!" Most folks love sharing their story, especially if you keep it short and sweet.

Once you've got some real info and a couple of stories from people in the trenches, it's time to doodle your own career map. Start by scribbling your top values and strengths at the top; think of them as your personal filter. Underneath, list two or three paths that sound interesting. For each one, sketch out two timelines: short-term (what you could try in the next year) and long-term (where you might end up in a few years). Maybe you start with a marketing contract while learning design on weekends, and down the road, you're running your own agency or working on strategy at a nonprofit. Don't be shy about drawing arrows all over the place; real careers rarely go in a straight line.

Career Compass Snapshot

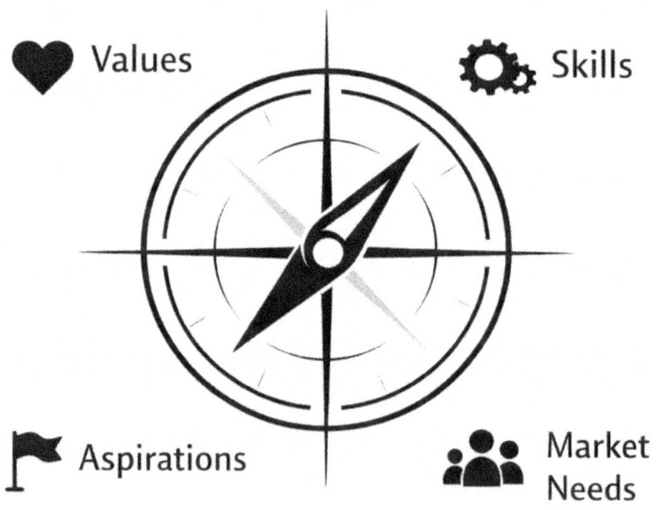

Before you pick a path and sprint down it, give yourself permission to take a few "test drives." You wouldn't buy a car without a spin around the block, right? So why jump into a job without a sneak peek? Try out short-term projects, do some volunteer gigs, or shadow someone for a day. Curious about content strategy but not ready to dive in? Offer to run social media for a local group. Want to dip your toes into tech? Sign up for a beginner hackathon or a micro-internship. These little experiments help you build skills, meet new people, and figure out what gets you excited, without locking yourself in for years.

Interactive Element: Career Map Worksheet

Create three columns: "Possible Paths," "Short-Term Moves," "Long-Term Moves." Fill each column based on what excites you most right now. Then circle the options that best align with your values and strengths from earlier. Keep this worksheet handy; you'll update it as you learn more or as your interests shift.

Every good career map looks a little messy, full of scribbles, crossed-out ideas, and random arrows. The more you treat your path like a living, breathing thing, the more likely you are to spot cool opportunities (and end up somewhere that fits). There's no one-size-fits-all way to build momentum. What matters is steering on purpose, not just floating along. Try things out in small doses before you go all in; your future self will be glad you did.

The Sustainable Success Equation: Progress Without Burnout

If you've ever found yourself answering emails at midnight, eyes glazed over and snack stash running dangerously low, thinking that just one more hour will finally earn you that magical "career gold star," you're in good company. Most of us have been lured in by the hustle culture anthem that says grinding nonstop is the only way to win. But here's the plot twist: Burnout is skyrocketing, especially for people early in their careers. It's not that we can't handle work; it's that no one teaches us how to do it sustainably. You don't have to be glued to your laptop 24/7 to get ahead. In fact, people who set boundaries and pace themselves usually end up doing better. Take a simple comparison: One person answers every ping at all hours and eventually fizzles out; the other blocks off time for deep work, takes real breaks, and logs off at the end of the day. The second one isn't slacking; they're just playing the long game. Think of it like marathon training: Sprint the whole way and you'll collapse halfway; keep a steady pace, and you might even finish with a smile.

Burnout rarely shows up all at once. It tends to build quietly in the background, especially when ambition, pressure, and "just push through it" thinking collide. Early in a career, it's easy to mistake chronic exhaustion for commitment or assume stress is simply part of proving yourself. Learning to notice when effort is outpacing recovery is a skill, not a weakness. We'll explore this in much more detail later in the book, including how to recognize early warning signs and protect your energy without hurting your career.

Setting boundaries before burnout takes hold doesn't require dramatic ultimatums; it starts with small, clear signals. If your boss drops a last-minute project on Friday at 4 p.m., try this email: "Thanks for sending this over. I want to give it the attention it deserves, so I'll tackle it first thing Monday." For teammates piling on extra tasks: "I'm at capacity right now but happy to revisit this next week after my current deadlines." If you're asked to join every meeting on your calendar, use: "I want to stay focused on my core projects; can we loop in via notes or an async update?" Scripts like these feel awkward at first, but they get easier with practice, and they show colleagues you respect your own time.

The real magic when taking care of yourself is in tiny, repeatable habits. Set a timer for mini-breaks every 90 minutes, stretch, wander around, or just zone out and stare at the wall like you're pondering the meaning of life. Before you log off, jot down one win and one thing you want to tweak tomorrow. On those wild weeks, try a "digital detox hour": phones off, notifications silenced, brain on chill mode. You'll be surprised how much clearer everything feels after a real break.

Accountability is a game-changer, too. Build your own "personal board of directors," aka a few friends, mentors, or coworkers who will check in and help you stick to your boundaries. Maybe it's a group chat where you swap goals on Monday and share wins (or faceplants) on Friday. These little support systems add up, making it much easier to say no when you need to and yes when it matters.

Sustainable routines might not sound as flashy as pulling all-nighters or chasing the latest productivity hack, but they add up fast. Take the designer who drew a hard line at 6 p.m. and refused to check Slack after hours. A few months later, her creativity was off the charts, and her boss noticed. Or the project manager who blocked out two hours every morning for deep work and started delegating the little stuff. He hit his deadlines with less stress and even squeezed in time for learning new skills. These aren't mythical creatures; they're just people who picked routines over chaos.

Rather than tracking every symptom or metric right now, focus on awareness and intention. Did you take a lunch break? Did you say no to something, even once? Celebrate those, because they're the real victories. These small choices are what build a career that grows strong and steady, without turning you into burnt toast.

Reflection prompt: Name one sustainability rule you'll put in place starting now. Maybe it's "no work after 7 p.m.," "one screen-free hour daily," or "weekends are for me." Write it down, then treat it like any important meeting on your calendar.

Setting Up Your Personal Dashboard: Tracking Growth and Well-Being

Nothing screams "I have my life together" quite like a dashboard. Well, maybe a color-coded spreadsheet or a thriving houseplant, but you get the idea. Jokes aside, setting up a simple system to track your growth, skills, and well-being is one of the smartest things you can do. Think of it as your career Fitbit: part tracker, part cheerleader, part "look at me go!" trophy shelf. You don't need to be a tech genius. Try Notion, Trello, or even a humble Google Sheet. The tool doesn't matter as much as making it your own and keeping it simple enough that you'll actually use it.

Start simple and build as you go. Your dashboard needs a spot for new skills you're learning (coding, public speaking, or finally figuring out how to fix the office printer); recent wins (nailed a tough project, got a shout-out from your boss, or just made it through a meeting without zoning out); and feedback, whether it's helpful, confusing, or somewhere in between. Make a section for your energy or mood, too. This is how you catch burnout sneaking up or spot what truly helps you thrive. Try tracking how you feel at the end of each week. Did you finish Friday ready to take on the world, or just desperate for pizza and quiet? Over time, you'll see what gives you energy and what drains it.

Minimum Viable Dashboard Setup Checklist

- Pick your platform (Notion, Trello, Google Sheets, whatever makes you smile).
- Make tabs or columns for skills, wins, feedback/notes, and energy/mood.
- Add a spot for quarterly goals (more on those in a minute).
- Choose one color or icon for "I crushed it!" moments and another for "needs work."

- Set a reminder to check in weekly; consistency beats fancy features.

SMART Quarterly Goals

Now, about those quarterly goals. Setting goals is a lot like flossing; everyone claims they do it, but most of us just wing it until something goes wrong. The trick is to make your goals **SMART: specific, measurable, achievable, relevant, and time-bound**. So, instead of "get better at presentations," try "give two team updates without reading from notes by the end of the quarter." For well-being, ditch the vague "stress less" and go for "take two 20-minute walks a week" or "block off one meeting-free afternoon every month." Every quarter, pull up your dashboard and check in: Which goals did you crush? Which ones need a little work? Where did you surprise yourself? Use prompts like, "What am I most proud of?" or "What challenge taught me the most?" This is your chance to course-correct before things go off the rails.

Don't forget to mix in well-being checks with your usual "look what I did!" moments. Sure, track the skills you built and the goals you hit, but also jot down how you felt along the way. Did that big project make you feel like a rock star, or did it send your stress levels into outer space? Was there a week when everything just clicked, or did you drag yourself through endless meetings? These notes matter a lot. If you spot your energy tanking or stress spiking for a few weeks in a row, that's your neon sign to make a change.

After a few months, your dashboard turns into your secret weapon for feedback chats and performance reviews. No more scrambling to remember what you did or why you deserve a raise; just pull up your dashboard and let the receipts do the talking. For example, "I finished X project early," "Three teammates gave me shout-outs," or "I automated reporting and saved us five hours a week." Real data beats wishful thinking every time, and it saves you from relying on your memory when the pressure's on.

If you're gearing up for a promotion chat or annual review, pull highlights straight from your dashboard. Point out patterns that show you're growing or bouncing back: "I picked up two new responsibilities since last time," or "My motivation tanked in March, but after tweaking my workload, my output jumped by 20%." Suddenly, you're not just talking yourself up, you're telling a clear story with real proof. It also makes self-advocacy less scary, because you're sharing facts, not just vibes.

A personal dashboard isn't just for overachievers or spreadsheet nerds; it's for anyone who wants to see real progress without losing their mind. Set it up in the simplest way possible and tweak it as you go. Your future self will thank you for having a real record of growth and balance, not just what you did, but how you felt along the way. That's how you build real momentum: not with giant leaps, but with steady steps and enough self-awareness to know when to push and when to chill.

Chapter 2

Skill-Building Roadmaps for Real-World Impact

Skill Audit: Pinpointing High-Leverage Abilities for Your Field

Nobody wants their skills to be the work version of dial-up internet: slow, unimpressive, and basically, begging to be replaced. If you've ever found yourself frantically collecting LinkedIn certificates or chasing every shiny new "must-have skill," you're not alone. But here's the thing: Getting strategic about what really matters in your field will save you a lot of time and headaches.

Start by doing a brutally honest inventory of your skills. Think of it like cleaning out your kitchen cabinets and finding that can of beans you forgot about. Write down everything you can do, from the everyday stuff (like wrangling your inbox) to the more specialized things (maybe you're the go-to for building a growth dashboard). Don't hold back or skip the basics. Once you've got your list, sort it out: Basic skills are the ones most people could pick up with a little training, while advanced skills are the ones that make you the person everyone calls when things get tricky (like launching a viral campaign or running successful A/B tests).

Skill Audit Overview

Skill	Level (Basic/Advanced)	Frequency of Use	Impact

Use this "Skill Stack" worksheet to get organized:

- **Column 1:** Skill
- **Column 2:** Basic/Advanced
- **Column 3:** Frequency of Use (Daily, Weekly, Rarely)
- **Column 4:** Impact (Low, Medium, High)

For example, "Writes weekly newsletter" might land in the basic, often-used, medium-impact zone, while "Sets up complex automation flows" is more like advanced, rare, and high-impact territory. Lining things up this way makes it easier to spot where your real superpowers are hiding.

Don't guess what skills matter most; research them. Job postings are invaluable for this. Check LinkedIn or Glassdoor for roles you aspire to, and note which skills are repeatedly mentioned. For example, a product marketing role might repeatedly list "customer journey mapping" or "SQL." Track these in your worksheet. Also, consult the

LinkedIn Talent Blog for their annual skill reports, which frequently highlight both evergreen essentials (communication, leadership, problem-solving) and field-specific "rising star" skills (like Python or workshop facilitation). Stay updated by setting Google Alerts, joining industry-specific forums or subreddits, and following recruiters on social media.

Cross-functional skills matter too. These let you pivot between teams or even industries. Studies from places such as Harvard Extension School show that adaptability and digital literacy are increasingly vital across the board. Screenshot job posts, highlight repeating requirements, and consolidate this data in your worksheet. For a shortcut, browse LinkedIn Learning or Indeed's trending skills lists.

Quick warning: It's way too easy to become a "badge collector," piling up courses and certificates until your résumé looks like a digital junk drawer. That's not the goal here. Ask yourself if each skill is actually helping you get better, or if it's just keeping you busy. Chasing every shiny new thing leads straight to burnout and a bunch of half-baked skills. Mastery and real, hands-on know-how will always beat a long list of things you barely remember.

How to prioritize what comes next? Apply the 80/20 rule: Focus on the 20% of skills that will yield 80% of your future opportunities. If you're a UX designer, for example, mastering workshop facilitation or behavioral data analysis does far more for your career than simply learning another wireframing tool. As a project coordinator, proficiency in process automation could quickly double your effectiveness and unlock advancement.

For extra clarity, make a self-assessment matrix. List your desired skills and rate your proficiency as red/yellow/green (beginner/intermediate/advanced). Add an "urgency" column for how crucial each skill is to your goals and market demand. For example, if you rate yourself as intermediate in public speaking but recognize its importance for promotions or client work, it jumps up your priority list, even over technical skills.

Interactive Element: High-Leverage Skill Snapshot

Give yourself five minutes to jot down one to three skills that check these boxes: in-demand, make a real difference in your job (or help you ask for a raise), and you're actually interested in them. These are your real priorities, not just whatever's trending on LinkedIn this week.

Take a second to ask yourself whether you are picking up skills that actually open doors, or just collecting buzzwords to sound impressive. When in doubt, focus beats quantity every time.

The T-Shaped Skillset: Balancing Depth and Breadth for Maximum Opportunity

Think of your skill set as a "T": The vertical line is your deep expertise in one area (say, being the go-to Excel or spreadsheet expert), while the horizontal bar represents a broad range of additional, useful skills (maybe knowing just enough about graphic design to give feedback or basic coding to avoid causing issues on the website). The T-shaped model keeps you from being boxed in or easily replaced; you become valued not just as a specialist, but as someone who can work effectively across teams, communicating with designers, troubleshooting with IT, and contributing to marketing brainstorms.

Take the example of a product manager whose deep expertise in UX design forms the vertical of their "T," while basic business strategy and enough technical know-how to converse with engineers and marketers round out the horizontal. This combination makes them a bridge-builder, someone who translates between teams, spots overlooked opportunities, and helps projects move forward without constant support. Managers love having T-shaped team members, coworkers rely on them, and recruiters seek them out.

T-Shaped Skill Stack

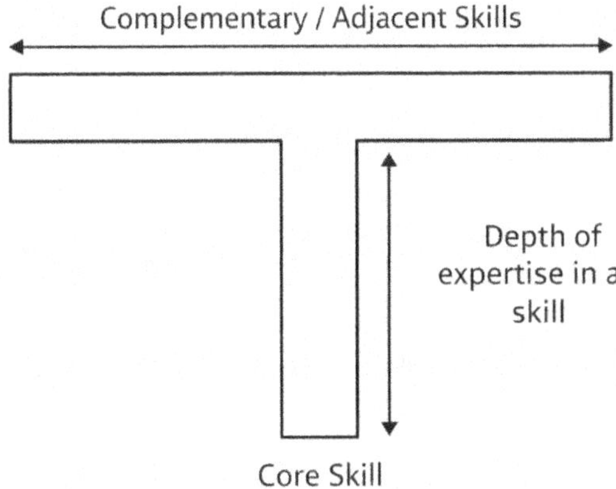

Mapping your own T-shape is straightforward and even fun. Start with a big "T" on paper or a tablet. Down the long vertical, write your core area of expertise, the skill you're known for and want to develop further. Across the top, list two or three additional skill areas that would make you more versatile. For example, if you're a developer, you might benefit from learning about client communication or basic project planning; if you're in HR, a little data analysis or content creation can help. Don't overthink it; just note the first things that come to mind.

Early in my career, I focused almost entirely on Excel. I wanted to be the person who could build clean spreadsheets, untangle messy data, and make numbers make sense. That worked well until I had to explain my work to managers or stakeholders who did not live inside spreadsheets. I realized pretty quickly that strong technical skills only got me halfway there. So I started practicing how to summarize insights, present findings in plain language, and walk people through what the numbers actually meant. My "T" grew wider not because I mastered everything, but because I stopped hiding behind spreadsheets and learned how to communicate what I already knew.

Go Beyond the Basics

To really level up your main skill, you've got to go past the basics. Find a mentor who pushes you, or pick a course that makes you sweat a little, not just one that looks good on your profile. If you're an analyst, try making your data visualizations so clear that even your grandma would get it. Side projects are perfect for this: Pick a real problem and see if you can solve it with a new tool or approach.

For the horizontal, adding breadth, don't try to master everything or overwhelm yourself. Look for cross-training that fits into your workflow. Cross-functional projects are a goldmine: Maybe you help marketing with a campaign or join a finance brainstorming session. Lunch-and-learn sessions are a low-pressure way to soak up new knowledge. If your company doesn't do these, start a peer learning group or a casual "teach me something" lunch, even remotely. Mini-projects, such as writing a couple of blog posts, analyzing customer data, or supporting a redesign sprint, offer exposure to new domains without requiring you to be an expert.

As you broaden your skill set, focus on complementary areas that refine your core strength and make team collaboration smoother. Engineers who learn a little about UI/UX streamline communication with designers. Finance professionals who pick up project management basics work better with operations or HR. Look for adjacent skills that frequently arise in meetings or slow down project handoffs; these are ripe for upskilling.

The payoff with T-shaped skills is that you become a connector, someone who sees the big picture and jumps into new roles when needed. Teams trust you'll ask smart questions, and leaders notice your ability to solve problems by merging ideas from various fields.

This approach makes you future-proof, not just for job promotions, but for whatever turns your career may take.

Quick Mapping Exercise

Grab your notebook or notes app and draw a "T." Down the middle, jot your deepest skill, the thing you want to be recognized for at work. Across the top, add at least two other fields where basic skills would improve your collaboration or open new doors. Circle one area to deepen this quarter and one to broaden. Revisit this sketch whenever you feel stuck or want to plan your next learning step.

Upskilling and Reskilling: Fast-Tracking Your Learning Without Feeling Overwhelmed

If you're eyeing a new role or itching for a raise, chances are you've been told to "upskill" or "reskill." Cool, but what does that look like when your calendar already feels like a game of Tetris? The secret isn't cramming every new skill into your week; it's learning with intention. Start with targeted goals that move the needle for your next career step. Don't just say, "I want to get better at Excel." Try, "I'll learn how to build automated dashboards in Excel by the end of the quarter so I can apply for that operations analyst role." SMART goals are specific, measurable, achievable, relevant, and time-bound. They turn fuzziness into focus. Say you're itching to shift from customer support to product management. Instead of drowning in generic business courses, you might set this goal: "Complete a beginner's agile product management course on Coursera and launch a mock product roadmap in Notion within eight weeks." This puts an actual finish line on your learning and ties it to a real outcome.

Where to Learn

Now, where do you learn without draining your bank account or sanity? There's no shortage of platforms out there, but not all are created equal. Coursera and LinkedIn Learning are solid for structured, up-to-date courses that employers recognize. Udemy is perfect for quick, affordable deep dives, like "SQL for Busy People" or "Figma in 48 Hours." Don't ignore YouTube; plenty of experts upload quality tutorials for free. If you'd rather learn with others and not go it alone, hunt down meetups, Discord groups, or Slack communities focused on your field. These spaces offer more than camaraderie; they provide support, accountability, and a chance to swap tips or resources in real time. Sometimes, the quickest way to learn is by asking someone in a chatroom, not combing through a fifty-page textbook.

Before you sign up for that shiny new certification, pause for a quick "Learning ROI Quick-Check." Ask yourself: *Will this skill help me get promoted, land interviews, or solve real problems at work?* Is it recognized in job postings you actually want? Does the course offer hands-on projects or just hours of passive video? How much time (and money) are you trading for this badge? If it doesn't check at least two of those boxes, skip it. There's no point in stacking digital trophies that don't open doors or boost your confidence.

Most of us don't have the patience or the free weekends for marathon study sessions. Instead, try the Pomodoro trick: Set a timer for twenty-five minutes, focus on one thing, then take a five-minute break. Do that a few times and call it a win. You'll be surprised how much sticks with short, focused bursts. Another hack is habit stacking. Sneak your learning into stuff you already do, like listening to a podcast on your commute or flipping through flashcards while you wait for your coffee. Little tweaks like this make learning more doable and less overwhelming.

People make wild moves in their careers with the right approach to upskilling, sometimes with less effort than you'd expect. Take Jamie, who went from teaching high school science to UX design in under a year. She set a monthly project-based goal: Redesign one nonprofit website per month using lessons from free online bootcamps. She joined a Discord group for peer reviews and built a portfolio filled with real projects, not just theory. Her new boss didn't care about her formal credentials; they hired her because she showed she could solve problems and work with feedback. Or consider Adam, who worked in operations at a SaaS startup but felt boxed in by repetitive tasks. Instead of jumping straight into another degree, he picked one analytics course and made a deal with his manager to automate the monthly reporting process as his "final project." That side project proved his growth mindset and landed him an internal move to data analytics.

The best thing about upskilling right now? Resources are everywhere, and many cost less than takeout. Just don't fall into the trap of trying to learn everything at once. Pick what moves you forward, break it into bite-sized chunks, and lean on communities for feedback and a little nudge when you need it. That way, you're not just hoarding knowledge; you're putting it to work in ways that matter.

Showcasing Skills in Action: Portfolios, Projects, and Proof

You don't need to be a designer or a coder to show off what you can do. These days, building a digital portfolio is for everyone: writers, marketers, HR pros, analysts, and even those in roles with zero design in the title. Think of your portfolio as the highlight reel of your career: It tells the story of what you've actually accomplished, not just what you claim on your résumé. The trick isn't just dumping every project you've ever touched into a folder and calling it a day. You want to be intentional, so managers see your real impact at a glance.

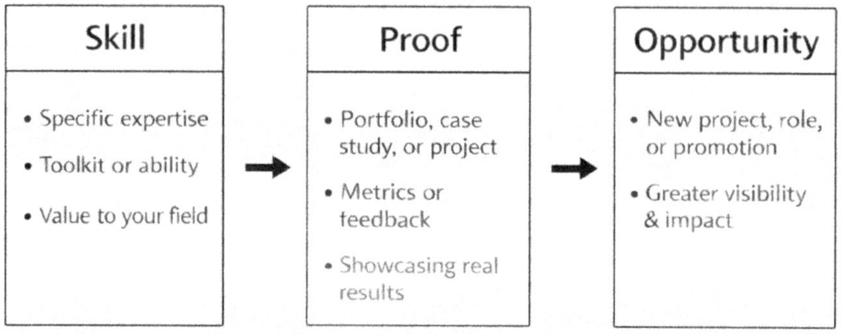

If you're starting from scratch, Notion or Google Drive are your best friends. Set up a simple folder system, one for each major skill or project type. For each item you add, include a brief description: what the project was, your specific role, and what changed because you were involved. Say you're a marketer: One folder could be "Social Campaigns," another "Email Optimization," maybe a third for "Analytics Wins." Attach samples, screenshots of campaign results, slides from presentations, and links to live work. Writers can drop in published articles or blog posts. HR folks might showcase onboarding guides they created or employee engagement initiatives they led.

Don't fall into the trap of only showing polished, perfect work. Sometimes the messiest projects are the ones where you learned the most or made the biggest difference. Select projects that show range, one that highlights creativity, another problem-solving, maybe a third that proves you can work under pressure or lead a team. When you're describing each project, skip the vague stuff ("helped with team goals") and get specific. Use the STAR framework to give your story structure: Situation (what was happening?), Task (what was your goal?), Action (what did you actually do?), Result (what changed?). For example: "Our website traffic was flat (Situation). I was asked to boost leads through content (Task). I launched a new blog series and promoted it with targeted ads (Action). Outcome: 35% increase in qualified leads over three months (Result)." Show before/after screenshots if possible; numbers always help.

Proof matters more than ever, especially if you're applying for roles where everyone seems to have the same qualifications. Attach actual evidence, screenshots of results, positive feedback from colleagues or clients, or even short testimonials, if you can get them. Quantify your outcomes wherever possible ("Reduced onboarding time by 20%," "Managed a $50K budget without going over," "Coached three interns who all got full-time offers"). If you've worked on something confidential or under NDA (Non-Disclosure Agreement), describe your process and outcomes in broad terms without sharing sensitive details. Consider including "project briefs" as PDFs or links directly on your LinkedIn profile or as part of your résumé attachments. More recruiters now want proof, not just promises.

Keeping your portfolio fresh is where most people trip up. Set a quarterly calendar reminder to review and update your work samples. This doesn't have to be a massive chore; scan for anything outdated, add one new project, and delete anything irrelevant to where you want to go next. If you're aiming for a promotion or career switch, focus your portfolio on skills and results that match your target role. Don't hesitate to create different versions for different types of jobs; marketing yourself is not one size fits all.

Portfolio Readiness Checklist

- Can someone tell at a glance what kind of work you do and what makes you different?
- Do your examples clearly show results, not just activity?
- Are all samples recent enough that they still reflect your current skills?
- Is your contact info easy to find?
- Have you added at least one new project or update in the past six months?

Think of this checklist like changing the oil in your car: Do it regularly so you don't end up stranded when a big opportunity rolls up.

Portfolios aren't just for job-hunting either. Use them in annual reviews to negotiate raises ("Here's proof I saved us money"). Pull out examples when you ask for new responsibilities or want to negotiate scope creep ("See how I handled that last-minute crisis?"). If someone asks what you do all day, send them your link instead of rambling through a list. You'll look prepared and confident, and who doesn't want that?

When you're not sure what to include, keep it simple and focus on what made a difference. Your portfolio should feel like a living scrapbook of what you've learned and accomplished, not just a digital brag board. The clearer you make your story, the easier it is for people to see your value and say yes when it matters.

Before diving deeper into soft skills, take a quick reality check. These skills are often assumed rather than intentionally developed, yet they quietly shape how your work is perceived and how far it travels. Read through the list below and be honest with yourself, not about what you want to be good at, but about what you consistently demonstrate at work.

Soft Skills Reality Check

Which of these are you using, not just claiming?

- I can explain my work clearly to non-experts.
- I listen without interrupting or rushing to fix.
- I adapt quickly when priorities change.
- I handle feedback without getting defensive.
- I manage my time without constant stress.
- I stay calm under pressure.
- I ask clarifying questions before making assumptions.

- I follow through consistently.
- I collaborate well across teams.
- I manage conflict without avoiding it.
- I communicate progress proactively.
- I take ownership when things go wrong.

You don't need to master all of these; even strengthening one clear boundary or soft skill can dramatically increase the impact of your technical abilities.

Soft Skills as Career Multipliers: Communication, Adaptability, and EQ

Soft skills don't show up in job postings, but they play a huge role in getting you noticed, promoted, and paid more, often faster than technical know-how alone. Companies highly value people who communicate clearly, adapt to change, and handle feedback without overreacting. Communication consistently tops "most wanted" skills lists. You want to make your point clear, truly listen, and ensure others feel heard. In meetings, that's summarizing what's been said or spotlighting next steps. On Slack or Teams, it means being concise, avoiding jargon, and getting to the point. The best communicators aren't always the most talkative; they're effective because their messages are understood.

Emotional intelligence (EQ) is a quiet superpower, especially in stressful situations. The coworker who remains calm during chaos? That's EQ at work. It helps you read the room, recognize stress, and respond thoughtfully rather than overreact. Feedback becomes a collaborative conversation, not an attack. On cross-functional teams, with shifting priorities and personalities, EQ makes you the go-to person for collaboration and problem-solving.

Tactical Tips

Before your next meeting or presentation, prep a few phrases to clarify and bring the group back to focus, for example, "Just to recap, here are our next steps..." or "Can we make sure we're aligned on timelines?" For tough feedback, keep things positive: "I noticed [specific action] had this impact. How can we approach it differently next time?" When conversations get heated, use active listening: Paraphrase what you've heard ("So you're saying...") and check for understanding. At first, it feels awkward, but it prevents misunderstandings.

Want real practice? Pick an upcoming conversation, whether with your boss, your team, or a friend, and choose one communication or listening skill to focus on. Maybe ask clarifying questions rather than giving advice, or pause before reacting to criticism. Jot down how it goes. For extra practice, role-play with a friend or record yourself to spot areas for improvement.

Adaptability is what separates "just okay" from "indispensable" professionals. Change comes constantly: new tools, changing goals, surprise layoffs. Adaptable people don't panic; they focus on the new goal instead of the old plan. Test yourself: Think of the last time you had to learn something quickly. How did you cope? Rate yourself from 1 (change-averse) to 5 (bring it on). Want to stretch? Volunteer for a task outside your comfort zone and treat it as adaptability practice.

Emotional regulation is another important skill. It involves staying grounded when situations frustrate or stress you, like being interrupted repeatedly or getting extra work right before the weekend. To pinpoint which soft skill is holding you back, communication, adaptability, or emotional regulation, reflect on recent work stressors. Where did things go wrong? Spot a pattern? Identifying weak spots is the first step to improvement.

Success Stories

Real stories speak louder than skill lists. Mia, for example, was quiet but reliable, listened well, and always delivered. When her team leader left unexpectedly, her listening and follow-through made her the natural choice for leadership, even outshining more vocal colleagues. Or take Ravi, who switched from journalism to tech sales by networking with empathy rather than cold pitches. By remembering details, sending thoughtful follow-ups, and asking genuine questions, his EQ built real relationships and job opportunities.

Soft skills may seem invisible, but they are the glue that holds teams together and the real driver behind promotions and pay raises, often outweighing any technical tool or trick. Next, we'll explore how to turn these abilities into lasting leverage so your growth never plateaus.

Chapter 3

Confident Communication in Modern Workplaces

The Feedback Loop: Giving, Receiving, and Asking for Constructive Input

Relying on annual reviews for feedback is like checking your GPS once on a cross-country road trip; by the time you realize you missed a turn, you're already in the wrong state. If you want to grow (and not just collect cryptic notes at the end of the year), you need real-time, specific feedback. The people who move up fastest? They're the ones who ask for input, do something with it, and then circle back for more. It's a loop, not a one-and-done. Regular feedback doesn't just keep you from guessing; it makes you more engaged, creative, and mobile in your career. Basically, it's like giving your progress a turbo boost without waiting for someone else's calendar.

Asking for feedback can feel about as natural as trying to fold a fitted sheet. But it gets easier if you keep it simple and specific. Worried you'll sound needy? Try direct, low-key questions. For email, you could say, "Hi [Manager/Peer], I'm working on getting better at [task]. Do you have one suggestion for me? Even something tiny helps." In meetings, go with, "What's one thing I could do differently to be more effective?" Sticking to just "one thing" keeps it from feeling overwhelming for the other person. If you're managing others, try, "I'd love your honest input. How can I support your work better?" Tweak the wording to fit your style, but keep it chill and focused.

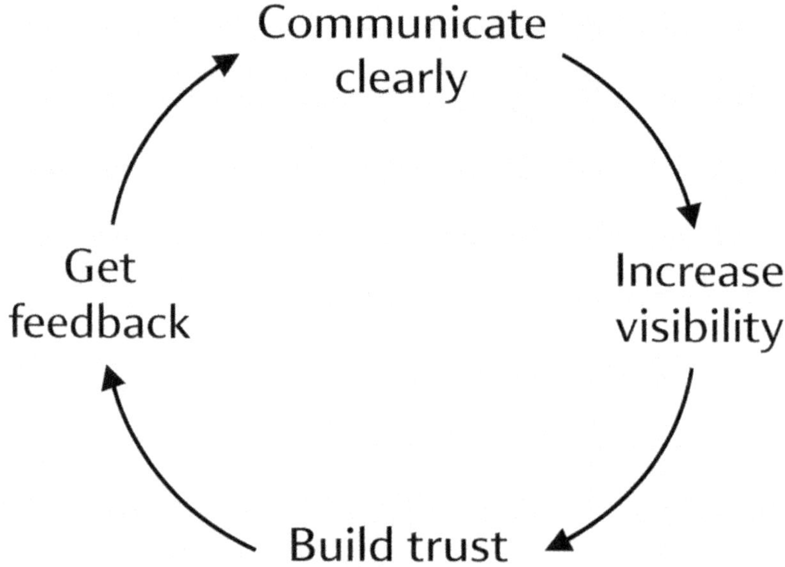

When giving feedback, especially upward or across teams, avoid blunt criticism like "You messed up that deadline." Instead, use the SBI framework: **Situation, Behavior, Impact**.

- Describe the situation neutrally. ("During yesterday's team meeting...")
- Name the specific behavior. ("...when the update wasn't shared...")
- Explain the impact. ("...it left the group unclear on next steps.")

This way, you skip the blame game and make it easier for the other person to focus on fixing things instead of getting defensive. For example: "In last week's sprint review (Situation), when the handoff was delayed (Behavior), it set the project back two days (Impact). How can we avoid that next time?"

Use SBI for positive feedback as well: "When you took the lead on the client call (Situation), your calm responses (Behavior) helped us quickly build trust (Impact)." If addressing unclear communication: "In the last report (Situation), some terms weren't defined (Behavior), so I got confused presenting it (Impact)." The more specific you are, the more helpful the feedback will be.

If you get feedback that's super vague or just feels a little harsh, like "show more initiative" or "be more visible," don't just nod and hope for the best. Ask for an example: "Can you give me a picture of what that would look like in my day-to-day?" or "When could I have shown that?" Jot down what they say, take a breather if you need to, and then break it into bite-sized actions. If "be more visible" turns out to mean sending a weekly update, set a reminder and actually do it.

Interactive Element: The Feedback Reflection Sprint

Grab your phone or a scrap of paper and write down a piece of feedback you've gotten, bonus points if it's from a random chat message. Next to it, jot down one thing you could do about it this week. For example:

Feedback: "Speak up more in meetings."

Action: "Prep one comment before each team call."

Tiny steps, done repeatedly, beat big dramatic gestures every time.

Getting feedback can sting, but reframing helps: Ask what change the person is hoping for.

Use this worksheet after tough feedback:

1. What did I hear?
2. When did it happen?
3. How did I react?
4. What small experiment can I try to address it?
5. When will I review my progress?

Even the pros get hit with tough feedback. The difference? They use it to level up instead of letting it wreck their confidence. If you keep the feedback loop going, you'll learn faster than the folks who just wait for the annual review. Plus, it shows everyone around you that you're flexible and hungry to grow, exactly the kind of stuff that gets noticed when promotions roll around.

Managing Up: Expectations, Boundaries, and Visibility

Managing up isn't just corporate buzzword bingo; it's your secret weapon for daily sanity and long-term progress. At its core, managing up means working smart *with* your boss, not just *for* them. You want to understand their goals, style, and headaches so you can help both yourself and your team win. If you're early in your career, especially in a remote or hybrid role where watercooler chats are mythical creatures, this skill is pure gold.

When you manage up, you turn "just another employee" into "trusted ally," someone who anticipates needs, clarifies confusion, and builds real trust. Think of the junior designer who noticed her manager was always scrambling before client meetings. She started sending a quick status email every Thursday, summarizing project progress and potential snags. Soon, her manager leaned on her as the team's go-to for clarity. She wasn't being a show-off; she was just being proactive with communication.

To get real alignment, you need frameworks that make expectations explicit instead of playing workplace mind reader. Try a weekly check-in note:

"Hey, [Manager], here's what I'm working on this week: [List 2–3 main tasks]. Anything I should shift or reprioritize?"

This approach nips confusion in the bud.

For monthly or quarterly priority meetings, throw out questions like:

- "What's the most important outcome for our team this month?"
- "How do you define success for this project?"

If you want to look extra sharp, confirm these three things before ending any alignment meeting:

- Your top priorities
- How success will be measured (metrics, deliverables)
- How often your manager prefers updates, email, Slack, or in-person

This quick "alignment snapshot" keeps everyone on the same page and gives you a reference when shifting priorities turns your to-do list into a game of Jenga.

Setting Limits

Boundaries are where things get messy. Nobody wants to be the office buzzkill, but if you say yes to every after-hours ping, your job turns into one of those never-ending group projects from college. The trick is to set limits without making it weird. If your manager asks for something late, try: "I want to give this the attention it deserves. I'll pick it up first thing tomorrow." If you're always on call, block out "focus" time on your calendar or set up a daily 30-minute window called "Quick Qs" so you can batch the interruptions instead of letting them hijack your whole day. Most managers are cool with clear boundaries as long as you keep delivering.

Being visible at work doesn't mean you have to become the office hype machine or cc: everyone and their dog on every little thing. It means sharing your progress and wins in a way that feels like you. For a long time, I assumed my work spoke for itself. Then I started sending a short email to my department every morning with a quick snapshot of the previous day's sales and one brief comment on what stood out. It felt unnecessary at first, but it quietly changed how visible and trusted my work became.

When you wrap up a big project or hit a milestone, send a quick "wins" email:

Hey, team, quick update: [Project name] went live today! We solved [key challenge], and early feedback looks good. Thanks for all the support!

This keeps the higher-ups in the loop and gives your teammates credit, too.

When review time comes, don't be shy about speaking up for yourself. Make a list of what you accomplished and tie it to real results ("Cut onboarding time by 20%," "Launched a dashboard that saved five hours a week"). Practice saying: "One thing I'm proud of this year is [achievement], which led to [result]." It's not bragging; it's just giving your boss the receipts they need to fight for your raise.

Getting noticed also means speaking up in meetings, but not just to hear your own voice. Ask a smart question or sum up the next steps: "Just to clarify, are we moving forward with [project/decision]?" If you're remote and leadership is basically a name in Slack, try sending a short weekly update: "Here's what got done this week, and here's what's next." These little updates add up and help you build a rep for being reliable and proactive, without turning into the person who thinks every tiny task deserves a parade.

Now pause for a second: Which of these visibility moves makes you cringe the most: sending a wins email, speaking up in meetings, or asking for clearer priorities? Pick just one to try this week. Maybe you prep a question before each meeting or finally send that first status update. Small steps add up to big changes. Managing up isn't about sucking up or playing office politics; it's about being open, building trust, and making sure you and your boss both look good when it matters.

Handling Difficult Conversations: Scripts for Conflict, Credit-Stealing, and More

Nobody wakes up excited for a tough conversation at work. Most of us would rather grit our teeth than call out a teammate who quietly takes credit for our ideas. But ignoring it is like pretending that weird noise in your car will just go away; it never does. Awkward talks pop up for all kinds of reasons: Someone hogs credit, a project goes sideways, or you run into microaggressions. Before you jump in, figure out what you really want: an apology, some clarity, or to make sure it doesn't happen again? This gut-check keeps you focused when things get tense.

If someone tries to take credit for your work, it's easy to stew in silence or complain to your group chat. But if you never say anything, you're basically telling everyone it's fine to ignore your efforts. Instead, go for a direct but friendly approach: "Hey [Name], I noticed my work on [project] didn't get mentioned in the meeting. Just wanted to make sure we're clear on who did what." For email follow-ups, keep it polite and specific: "Hi [Name], can we make sure roles are clear next time? I contributed [specific part], and I'd appreciate that being noted in future updates." Figure out if this was a one-time slip or if it keeps happening. A gentle nudge usually fixes it, but if it's a pattern, you'll need a bigger game plan.

Not every conflict is a soap opera; sometimes it's just two people seeing things differently. Stick to "I" statements so you don't sound like you're pointing fingers: "I felt confused when the deadline changed at the last minute because I needed more time to adjust my part." Talk about your experience, not what they did wrong. If things are murky, try spelling out what you saw and how you took it: "When you updated the plan without looping me in, I figured my input didn't matter. Was that what you meant?" Most of the time, people don't even realize how their actions come across.

When you and a teammate disagree on direction, skip passive-aggressive emails and propose a direct conversation: "Can we talk about our goals for this project? I see benefits in [your approach], but I'm curious about your angle." Ask for their reasoning; you might find common ground, or at least understand their point of view. If you are clashing with a manager, acknowledge their broader responsibilities: "I know you have the big picture in mind, but I'm feeling stuck on [specific issue]. Could we brainstorm a workaround?" Framing it as a shared problem helps lower defenses.

Keep Your Receipts

Sometimes, no matter what you do, things just don't get better. That's when it's time to escalate, but you'll want your receipts. Keep track of dates, times, what was said or emailed, and what you did to try to fix things, especially if it's about credit, exclusion, or anything sketchy. Write down who was involved, what happened (with details or quotes), what you did, and how they responded. This isn't being petty; it's just looking out for yourself and making sure you have a clear record if you need to go to HR or higher-ups.

If escalation becomes necessary, don't panic. Stay factual and professional in your communication. A sample email: "Hi [HR/Manager], I wanted to bring to your attention ongoing issues regarding [brief description]. Despite addressing this directly with [Name] on [dates], there hasn't been any change. Can we discuss possible solutions?" Focus on facts rather than feelings, and suggest next steps if appropriate.

Tough conversations are never fun in the moment, but dodging them just leads to bigger headaches: missed chances, simmering resentment, and getting stuck in place. The good news? Every time you face conflict head-on (with a little tact), you get better at it. Awkwardness fades, but the progress sticks around, and sometimes, handling things well even earns you more respect.

Quick Reflection Sprint

Think back to a recent moment at work that made you uncomfortable: missed credit, a snarky remark, or confusion. Was it a one-time thing, or does it keep happening? Jot down one thing you wish you'd said and the outcome you'd want next time. Even rehearsing this boosts your confidence and prepares you for future challenges.

Navigating Remote and Hybrid Norms: Making Your Voice Heard

Remote and hybrid work have flipped many office basics on their head. Suddenly, just showing up and nodding in meetings isn't enough to prove you exist, unless your cat crashes your Zoom call. The truth? Visibility gaps are real. Research shows remote workers often get skipped over for recognition and promotions just because they're "out of sight, out of mind." If you've ever wrapped up a big project and felt like it vanished into the digital void, you're definitely not alone.

Quick gut check: If someone outside your team looked at last month's updates, would they have any clue what you did? If you're thinking, *probably not,* don't stress. Even one small move, like sending a weekly recap or dropping a project summary in the group chat, can put you back on the radar.

Staying visible without being that person is all about working smarter with async tools. Slack, Teams, and project boards are perfect for sharing progress, but there's a trick to writing updates people actually want to read. Skip the essay and keep it short and useful. A solid Slack update could look like:

Quick update: Completed the onboarding guide draft, sent to Sarah for review. Next up: integrating feedback by Friday. Blockers: waiting on marketing copy.

This tells everyone what's done, what's next, and what's needed, without anyone's eyes glazing over. For daily or weekly standups, try the "Three Bs" method:

Blocked (any obstacles?), **B**usy (what's in progress?), **B**oom (what did you finish?). Example:

Boom: Finished Q2 analysis. Busy: Drafting slide deck for client call. Blocked: Need numbers from Ops.

If you want to make it a habit, set a calendar reminder every Friday to drop a quick progress post, keep it light, and toss in a meme if your team's into that. Do this enough, and you'll stay on everyone's radar no matter where you're working from.

Looking Good in Virtual Meetings

Virtual meetings are their own brand of weird: awkward silences, people talking over one another, cameras off, and everyone secretly checking email. If you want to stand out (even if your video's off because your Wi-Fi is plotting against you), prep is your best friend. Ten minutes before the call, jot down two things you want to say and one question about the agenda. That way, when it's your turn, you're not left scrambling or just echoing, "I agree with what everyone else said." After the meeting, send a quick summary to the group or your manager:

Here's a quick recap from today's call. Action items: James will send the draft by Wednesday; I'll gather feedback on slides by Friday; next check-in set for Monday.

This not only makes you look organized, but it also makes sure nobody forgets what you actually did.

Trying to build work relationships from a distance can feel like yelling into the void. But digital connections are totally possible; you just have to get a little creative. Start by inviting someone to a 15-minute virtual coffee chat:

Hey [Name], I'd love to hear more about what you do here! Up for a quick virtual coffee next week?

No agenda needed; talking about weekend plans or your latest TV binge totally counts as networking these days. For a more casual connection, jump into "water cooler" channels or threads; even dropping a meme or asking for podcast recs helps break the ice. A quick "Congrats!" or "That's awesome!" when someone posts a win goes a long way and doesn't feel forced.

Getting to Know the Remote Team

Onboarding remotely? The first days are tricky when you can't pop by someone's desk or eavesdrop on team banter. Accelerate your credibility by introducing yourself proactively in chat channels:

Hi, all! I'm [Your Name], new to the [Team]. Super excited to jump in. If anyone has tips on [project/tool], send them my way!

Then, set up a few short calls with teammates just to find out what they do and how you'll be working together. When you hit your first project milestone, share it with the group; it shows you're taking initiative and helps everyone put your Name to real results.

To keep the momentum, pick one habit, like a Friday status post or a monthly "virtual lunch," and stick with it for a month. Make a note of what helps you feel more connected and what totally flops, so you can tweak as you go. The right habits make you visible and make remote work less lonely and a lot more fun.

High-Stakes Presentations and Meetings: Building Poise and Impact

Walking into a big meeting or gearing up for a high-stakes presentation can feel like you're about to jump off the high dive with everyone watching (and maybe judging your form). The upside? Anyone can look more confident and make an impact with a few simple tricks. Start with a clear structure: a strong opener (think story, stat, or even a perfectly timed meme), a middle with no more than three main points, and a close that people will actually remember. Don't drown your audience in data soup; pick one story or example for each point to make it stick. The "rule of three" is your friend; people remember things in threes, so use that rhythm for your main ideas.

When it comes to slides, less is always more. Go for big fonts, punchy headlines, and visuals that do the heavy lifting, charts, infographics, or even a funny GIF if it fits your team's vibe. Skip the walls of text; if your slide looks like a legal contract, people will tune out fast. Stick to one idea per slide and use color to highlight what matters. Before you call your slides done, pause and ask yourself: If people only remember one thing from this whole talk, what should it be? Jot it on a sticky note above your screen while you prep. This little trick keeps you focused and stops you from wandering off track.

Even the pros get nervous before presenting. The trick is to channel those jitters with a few easy moves. Try a grounded stance: feet shoulder-width apart, shoulders back, and take a couple of slow breaths before you start. Picture yourself nailing it, making eye contact, hitting your points, and seeing people nod along. These little rituals help you look and feel more confident. And during the meeting, keep your hands where people can see them (not stuffed in your pockets or hiding behind your laptop); it makes you look more open and in control.

Getting hit with tough questions can feel like playing dodgeball in work clothes. The trick? Don't rush your answer. Pause, nod, and say, "That's a great question. Let me think about that for a second." If you don't know, it's totally fine to say, "I'll need to check on that and get back to you," or steer things back with, "That's outside what we're covering right now, but I can follow up if it's important." If someone tries to interrupt or take over, just say, "Let me finish this point, and then I'll come back to your question." It keeps things moving without coming off as rude.

After every big meeting or presentation, take five minutes for a quick self-check. What seemed to land with people? Did you spot any light-bulb moments? What would you change next time? Jot down a few notes while it's still fresh so you can keep getting better, no over-thinking required.

Keeping a diverse audience engaged, whether it's a remote team spread across time zones or people from all sorts of backgrounds, takes a little extra effort. Use language everyone gets: Swap "guys" for "everyone," skip the jargon unless you explain it, and pick examples that make sense to your crowd. For remote groups, keep things lively with quick polls ("Which solution would work best for your team?"), invite chat reactions ("Drop an emoji if this hits home"), or share your screen for a live demo. If you're presenting to people in other coun-tries, double-check local customs: Will your joke land? Are there holi-days or time-zone quirks to watch for? A little prep goes a long way and shows you care.

Before you hit "present," do a quick tech check: Make sure your slides load, your mic works, and your background isn't showing off your laundry pile. Keep backup notes handy in case your Wi-Fi decides to act up. And always have water nearby, because dry mouth is no joke.

Bottom line: Clear structure always wins over rambling, visuals should help (not drown out) your words, and confidence comes from small tweaks and practice. You don't have to be perfect; just show up prepared and actually be there.

Chapter 4

Salary Negotiation Without Anxiety

Know Your Worth: Researching Compensation and Market Data

Let's set the scene: You're gearing up for a salary talk, and your well-meaning friend chimes in with, "Just ask for what feels fair." Nice in theory, but your gut could be off by a mile (or a few thousand dollars). Guessing your way through a negotiation is a recipe for regret. The folks who actually walk away happy? They do their homework. Real numbers beat office gossip every time, and you can load up on solid compensation data with a few smart searches and the right questions.

First stop: the big-name salary sites. Glassdoor, Payscale, and Levels are your new best friends. Glassdoor is like the Yelp of paychecks, crowd-sourced numbers by job title, city, and company. Payscale lets you slice and dice by experience, education, and skills. Levels is a must if you're eyeing tech giants like Google or Netflix. Don't just trust one site; compare a few to spot any weird outliers. Want to get extra nerdy? Check out public salary disclosures in states that require transparency, or poke around sites like H1BData.info for tech roles.

Some states, like New York and California, now make companies post salary ranges in job ads, so grab that info wherever you can.

But don't stop at websites. Your network is a goldmine for real-life salary scoop. Jump into Slack groups in your field and keep an eye out for pay threads. LinkedIn isn't just for humblebrags; try messaging people in similar roles at other companies and ask if they're open to swapping notes on pay ranges. (A simple, friendly message usually works wonders.) You'd be surprised how open people get about money, especially on anonymous forums like Blind.

Market Data Reality Check

Use these prompts to assess your research:

- Are you referencing at least two reputable salary sites for your target role?
- Have you checked recent job postings for pay ranges?
- Have you asked peers or connections about current compensation trends?
- Do your figures reflect both local and remote opportunities?
- Are you comparing roles with precise titles (not broad categories like "Manager" versus "Senior Manager")?

If you're missing any of these, take a few minutes to fill in the blanks; future you (and your bank account) will thank you. Waiting around for someone to magically notice you're underpaid? Yeah, that almost never happens.

Once you've got your numbers, stack them up against your role, industry, location, and experience. Paychecks can swing wildly; a project manager in Boston biotech is living a different reality than one at a nonprofit in Ohio. Regional quirks can mean a difference of tens of thousands of dollars, so don't forget to run offers through a cost-of-living calculator, especially if you're thinking about moving.

Company size matters too: Startups might dangle equity instead of cash, while big companies often have pay bands that don't budge much.

Don't just zero in on the base salary; peek under the hood at the whole package, including bonuses, stock options, RSUs, profit-sharing, signing bonuses, and the works. One company might offer $85K plus a 10% bonus and some RSUs, while another flashes $95K with nothing extra. The bigger number looks better at first, but those extras can tip the scales. Lay out the details side by side: Base Salary | Bonus | Equity | Perks | Total Value. Focus on what genuinely matters to you, not just the flashiest perk in the pile.

Decision Filter

Does this move build leverage?

Does it align with my long-term direction?

Does it cost me more than it gives?

Summarize your findings into an **"ask range,"** the bracket where you'd be happy to land. Use a spreadsheet or notepad for your compensation worksheet:

1. Note the low, median, and high figures from your research.
2. Adjust based on your experience and qualifications.

3. Factor in valuable non-cash perks (flex hours, remote work, education budgets, etc.).

By the end, you'll have three magic numbers: your target (the dream offer), your acceptable (the one you can live with), and your walk-away (the absolute lowest you'll take before you start plotting your escape).

Anchoring and Negotiating Your Starting Salary

Here's a pro move: anchoring. That's just a fancy way of saying you share your preferred range first, which puts you in the driver's seat. If the market says $60K–$80K, aim near the top: "Based on my research and experience, I'm targeting $78–$85K in total compensation." Anchoring high (but not wild) nudges the offer up.

Interactive Element: Market Range Snapshot

- My research says my target comp is: $_________
- I'll accept: $_________
- My walk-away number is: $_________
- The most common range for my role/company/location:
- $_________ – $_________

Keep this cheat sheet close when you're negotiating; it's your secret weapon for sounding confident (even if you're sweating through your shirt).

Negotiation isn't about bluffing or hoping you get lucky; it's about showing you know your worth because you did the homework. When you talk numbers instead of rumors, you come across as confident and credible, which is exactly what employers want to see.

Plug-and-Play Negotiation Scripts: From Offer to Counter-Offer

When you get a job offer, excitement often mixes with nerves. You might want to say yes quickly, especially after a long job search or if you're eager to leave your current job, but now's your chance to advocate for yourself. You don't need legalese or a TED Talk, just straightforward scripts and a little prep. Start with gratitude: "Thank you so much for the offer. I'm genuinely excited about the role and the chance to join your team." Use this opener whether you're responding by email, Slack, or phone. Then smoothly introduce your negotiation: "After reviewing the offer and considering my experience and market data, is there flexibility to discuss the base salary?" This approach is simple, direct, and friendly. If you're negotiating by phone or video, use pauses to your advantage. Silence here is powerful; it often prompts the other side to respond, sometimes with a better number.

If you need something more formal and more common with larger companies or talking to HR, try this adaptable email template:

Hi [Name],

Thank you again for the offer. I appreciate your team's investment throughout this process. I'm very enthusiastic about the position and see a strong fit between my background in [A] and your team's goals. Based on my research and experience, I was hoping we could explore a base salary in the [$B–$C] range. I believe this reflects both the market value for the role and what I'd bring to the team. Please let me know if there's room to discuss this further.

There's no need to write a novel or beg for mercy; the template is short, clear, and backed by real numbers.

For an internal raise, modify your opening:

Hi [Manager],

Thank you for discussing my performance and future here. In light of increased responsibilities and current market trends, I'd like to discuss a salary adjustment in line with industry benchmarks. I'm confident this will support strong results for our team.

No matter how you do it, keep things upbeat and treat the conversation like you're working together, not squaring off in a boxing ring.

Pick your script based on what feels right. Email is perfect if you want to lay out your points clearly or need a minute to collect your thoughts, as well as great for introverts or anyone who gets tongue-tied. Phone or video calls are better if you want instant feedback and a more personal vibe, plus you can adjust on the fly. If the back-and-forth drags on (which happens a lot), don't be afraid to switch it up: Start with an email, then hop on a call to iron out the details.

Negotiation relies as much on psychology as on wording. Use framing: Approach your request as finding a solution together ("How can we make this work for both of us?"). Try mirroring: Repeat their key phrases to show alignment ("You mentioned strong collaboration is important; I see my background adding value there"). Pauses are particularly useful; after you ask, be silent and let them consider. This pause creates space for them to move.

Negotiating from afar or across time zones? You'll need to tweak your approach. For email or Slack, be extra clear: Say what you want, why it matters, and what should happen next. Bullet points are your friend, but don't let your message sound like it was written by a robot. Keep it friendly.

It's normal to fear "What if they pull the offer?" but, in reality, that rarely happens; offers are rescinded in less than 3% of negotiations, and typically for fraud or extreme demands, not polite requests. Hiring managers expect negotiation. They may act surprised, but often it's just part of the tactic. If someone seems caught off guard, remain calm: "I understand this may be unexpected; I'm just hoping to find a package that works for both sides." If they flatly refuse, don't panic. Instead, see if there's flexibility on timing ("Could we revisit this after six months?") or if other benefits can be improved.

Negotiation is just part of the hiring dance, not some high-stakes showdown. With these scripts and a little prep, you'll walk in with confidence and probably walk out with a better deal than you thought possible.

Benefits, Equity, and Beyond Base Salary

Base salary is only part of the compensation picture; beneath it lies a world of perks, benefits, and "total rewards" that significantly impact your finances and lifestyle. Focusing solely on base pay can mean missing out on added value and a better quality of life.

Health insurance is a major factor: Always check coverage, costs for common services, and whether dental and vision are included. Extras like mental health support, wellness stipends for therapy or fitness, and even meditation apps can add meaningful value, especially if you regularly use them. Newer perks might include remote work stipends, professional development budgets for courses, and even funds to upgrade your home office setup.

Flexibility is the new gold. Remote work, extra PTO, or flexible hours can be just as valuable as a bigger paycheck. A job that pays $5,000 more but drags you into a daily commute might not beat one that lets you work in sweatpants and covers your Wi-Fi bill. Don't forget to count the savings on time, gas, and your sanity.

Before you negotiate, figure out what matters most to you. Maybe you care more about student loan help than a fancy title, or maybe pet insurance is your hill to die on. Focus on the perks that fit your life, not just what sounds impressive on paper.

When you're negotiating, don't get tunnel vision on salary. Use simple, direct questions to talk about other perks: Ask about start date wiggle room, remote work policies, learning stipends, bigger signing bonuses, or more vacation days. If you're moving, just ask straight up about relocation help. If the salary talks hit a wall, see what else you can nudge up.

Equity and stock options are common, but they are often confusing. Equity provides company ownership. Stock options allow you to buy company shares at a set price in the future, while RSUs (restricted stock units) are shares awarded after meeting certain conditions, like staying with the company for three years. Vesting schedules determine when you own those shares; for example, you might receive 1,000 RSUs over four years, with nothing received in the first year ("cliff"), and then 25% granted each year until you're fully vested. Leave before then, and you forfeit unvested shares, so don't overvalue future options.

When you're weighing offers, make yourself a quick grid: Base Pay | Health | PTO | Remote | Stipends | Equity | Perks. Fill in the blanks and see which perks matter to you right now (and which ones are just nice-to-haves for later). Maybe a startup pays $10K less but hands you a chunk of stock options. Just make sure the company isn't about to go belly-up. Sometimes cash is king, and sometimes equity wins, but the key is knowing what's right for you.

Benefits Prioritization Checklist

Rank these by importance (1 = must-have; 5 = nice-to-have):

- Health/dental/vision ____
- PTO/holidays ____
- Remote/flex work ____
- Student loan help ____
- Signing bonus ____

- Professional development funds ____
- Equity/stock/options ____
- Childcare/pet insurance ____
- Wellness/mental health support ____

Your priorities will shift over time. New grads usually chase loan help and cash, parents might need flexible hours or childcare, and seasoned pros may be eyeing long-term equity or a shot at leadership. What matters most now might change in a year, and that's totally normal.

To illustrate, consider Tony, a new grad with significant student debt. One job offers a slightly higher base; another includes $300 monthly for loan payments plus a learning stipend. The second offer might be more valuable to Tony in the long term, even with a lower base. Josie is mid-career and seeking a work-life balance, so she prefers flexibility and funds for professional development over a small pay bump.

Negotiating benefits is about creating a sustainable, satisfying career, not greed. Use direct language: "Given my background and current trends, could we discuss additional wellness stipends?" or "Would increasing the development budget be possible?" If one request is denied, remain positive and look for adjustments elsewhere.

Always look at the whole offer, not just the flashiest number. Weigh everything against what matters to you, both now and down the road.

Handling Pushback: What to Say When They Say "No"

It's a special kind of awkward when you finally get up the nerve to negotiate, only to hear a polite but firm "Sorry, this is the best we can do." Maybe they're stone-faced, or maybe they're apologetic, but the answer still feels like a door slamming shut. Here's the truth: Hearing "no" isn't a sign you've messed up. It's as common as coffee breath in morning meetings.

The next move is what sets you apart from everyone who simply shrugs and accepts. If you hit a wall, you don't have to fold. Acknowledge their position, "I understand your constraints," then keep the conversation rolling with, "Is there any flexibility to revisit this discussion in six months?" or "What can we do to close the gap between the offer and my expectations?" Sometimes all it takes is showing you're willing to compromise and keeping things positive. You open the door to possibilities even when a flat-out raise isn't on the table right now.

If salary is locked tighter than a bank vault, shift your focus. Ask about adjustments that make your life better, even if your paycheck stays the same. Additional paid time off, more remote days, a fancier job title, or early eligibility for review can all be on the menu. Professional development stipends are another card to play: "Would it be possible to support my attendance at an industry conference?" Even if you hear "no" on money, you might unlock budget for training or tech upgrades. Sometimes managers just need a gentle nudge to get creative. Don't be shy about suggesting options: "If salary can't move, could we add one extra remote day or revisit my title?" You'd be surprised how often these "small" wins add up.

When to Push and When to Pause

Now, knowing when to push versus when to pause is tricky. If the company genuinely can't budge, repeated asks won't win points. Instead, read the room: If their tone softens and they offer alternatives, listen carefully; there could be hidden gems in their offer. But if you sense resistance or irritation, it's smart to park the issue for now. Ask for a written note confirming when you'll next review your compensation. This puts your progress on record and gives you leverage later.

On the other hand, if an offer is far below your research or your minimum needs, don't be afraid to walk away. Your skills, energy, and time are valuable. Politely decline with gratitude: "I appreciate your time and consideration. If circumstances change, please keep me in mind." It's better to hold out for something right than say yes out of fear.

If you're stuck between sticking it out or running for the hills, try a quick decision matrix. Write down your must-haves, salary, flexibility, and growth, and score each offer (or counter-offer) against them. If everything comes up short, don't talk yourself into settling just because it's on the table. Trust your research and trust your gut.

Stories from real life help here: Plenty of candidates have turned down an offer after hitting a wall in negotiation, then left things on such good terms that the company came back months later with a higher budget and better benefits. A polite "no" isn't always the end; sometimes it's just a well-timed pause. Always leave doors open. Use language like, "I respect your decision and appreciate the transparency. Should things shift in the future, I'd love to reconnect." That phrase is magic; it keeps your reputation strong and sometimes gets you back in the running when budgets change.

Dealing with pushback is as much about your mindset as it is about your strategy. Don't let a "no" feel like a personal rejection or the end of the road; it's usually just a speed bump, not a brick wall. Staying calm and flexible shows real maturity, and hiring managers remember that. Even if this round doesn't go your way, you've planted seeds for next time, or at least avoided becoming an HR horror story. Every negotiation, win or lose, makes you better for the next one. And when you finally get that "yes," it'll feel even sweeter knowing you didn't fold at the first sign of trouble.

Negotiating as a Career Changer, Remote Worker, or Entry-Level Pro

Walking into a negotiation when your path isn't the so-called "normal" one, maybe you're switching fields, working from a new city, or just snagging your first real job, can feel like showing up to a potluck with a bag of chips while everyone else brought homemade lasagna. But here's the secret: If you know how to play up your strengths and ask smart questions, you can still leave with a plate piled high.

If you're changing careers, transferable skills are your biggest advantage. You might not tick every box on the posting, but the trick is to connect the dots for them. If you're moving from teaching into customer success, roles focused on helping clients use a product effectively and solve problems, don't downplay your classroom days. Instead, say, "While my experience is rooted in education, I've built expertise in communication, problem-solving, and managing groups, all directly relevant to supporting clients and resolving their issues." Drop in a concrete example: "For instance, I led a project where I streamlined parent communications, reducing response time by 30%." You're not asking them to take it on faith; you're showing the receipts. When you frame your story this way, you highlight how your unique background brings a fresh perspective, and you're not just "filling a gap"; you're expanding your team's range.

If they push back with, "But you haven't worked in SaaS before," pivot to your quick learning curve: "True, but I've consistently adapted to new tools and platforms, and I'm eager to jump in and get ramped up."

Remote work negotiations have their own quirks. Companies often adjust pay based on location, especially if you're moving from a high-cost city to somewhere more affordable, or vice versa. This can feel dicey: Suddenly, your offer is $10K lower because you swapped Brooklyn for Boise. Here's how to approach it: Start with gratitude for the opportunity, then go for transparency. "I understand the company adjusts compensation by location, but my experience and performance level remain unchanged. Can we discuss how my contributions align with the higher end of your range, regardless of city?"

If you're relocating but taking on more responsibilities or covering odd hours due to time zones, bring that up too: "While I'll be based remotely, I'll be supporting teams across three time zones. How does that factor into compensation?" You don't have to accept a pay cut just because your rent dropped; value is value.

Sometimes, remote workers flip the script entirely. Take someone who moved from a big city to a quieter (read: cheaper) town but then took on global projects or extra scope. They negotiated a raise by documenting increased impact and market rates for their expanded duties. Location wasn't the lever; contribution was. Don't hesitate to do the same.

Now, early-career pros, especially those eyeing entry-level roles, often assume their offers aren't up for debate. That's a myth. Most companies leave room for negotiation, especially for promising candidates. Rather than demanding a CEO salary in your first job, you're asking smart questions and nudging things upward.

Start by expressing excitement about the offer and then inquire about growth support: "What professional development resources are available for new team members?" or "Is there flexibility on starting salary or a signing bonus?" Even if base pay is firm, companies might sweeten deals with signing bonuses, relocation help, or early review cycles.

For those worried about seeming "difficult" right out of the gate, data shows entry-level offers are negotiated and improved more often than you might expect. Companies budget for it. One new grad I know asked about tuition reimbursement during her offer discussion and ended up with both a small signing bonus and company-paid certification courses, wins she'd have missed if she'd just said yes immediately.

If you're not sure what to say when you lack direct experience or are in a brand-new field, use this script:

My background is in [Z], but I've consistently demonstrated [skill] through [project/achievement]. I'm confident those skills will help me drive results here.

This keeps the focus on what you do bring to the table instead of what you haven't done yet.

Negotiating isn't just for the old pros or people with flawless resumes. It's for anyone who knows what they bring to the table and can connect their story to what the company really needs. Whether you're making a big career leap, working from your couch, or saying yes to your first offer, your approach matters. A little confidence (and a little homework) can help you bridge the gap between where you are and where you want to end up. Stand tall (even if you're in pajama pants on Zoom), own what you bring, and keep moving forward. Next up, we'll dive into using your network and building connections that open doors without forced small talk. I promise.

Chapter 5

Networking for Digital Natives and Introverts

Mapping Your Network: Hidden Connections and Relationship Leverage

You're awkwardly balancing a plate of mystery appetizers at some party when someone pipes up, "You remind me of my old roommate who works in your dream field." You laugh it off, but fast forward, and suddenly you're prepping for an interview thanks to that random connection. Networking feels like some kind of wizardry, but here's the real secret: Most of the good stuff doesn't happen at glitzy events or with perfectly rehearsed elevator pitches. It's hiding in your everyday circles, friends, friends-of-friends, even that person you only know from meme exchanges. The trick? Start by mapping out who you know.

Grab a piece of paper (or your tablet, if you're feeling fancy) and plop your name right in the middle. Now, start drawing lines out to everyone you can think of: friends, family, that one classmate you always run into at the grocery store, coworkers, neighbors, gym buddies, teammates, and yes, even your favorite barista if you've ever chatted about more than just your coffee order. Don't worry about job

73

titles, just jot down names. You'll probably be surprised how fast the page fills up. Then, start connecting the dots between people who know each other, like your college roommate who somehow ended up interning with your cousin's friend. Suddenly, you'll start to notice patterns, and those so-called "weak ties," the people you mostly know from meme swaps or the occasional community event, start popping up all over the place.

Here's the wild part: Those "weak ties" are goldmines for new opportunities. Because they're not in your usual crew, they can open doors to jobs, events, or advice you'd never stumble across on your own. So don't write off that friend-of-a-friend from your hiking group, or the classmate you haven't seen since high school who's now running a nonprofit. Sometimes those random connections go much deeper than you'd ever expect.

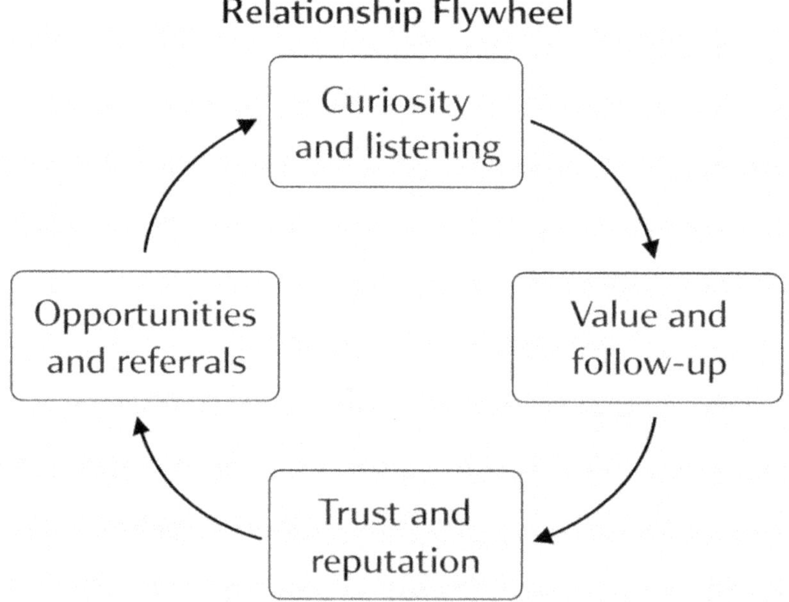

Relationship Flywheel

If you want to get a little more organized (and maybe feel like you're starring in your own detective movie), try color-coding or tagging your network. Maybe red for people in your field, blue for folks who could help you get hired, and green for those super-connectors who always seem to know someone. If you're a spreadsheet person, add columns for "industry," "influence," and "helpfulness." The point isn't to win some popularity contest; it's just a way to focus your energy so you're not blasting the same message to everyone you've ever met.

Now, let's talk about leverage, the not-scary kind! If you're eyeing a new field or want to talk to someone who feels totally out of reach, check your map: Who do you know that knows them? This is where "warm introductions" save the day. Just reach out to your mutual contact with a quick, friendly message:

Hey, Chris! I noticed you're connected with Jordan at [Company]. I'd love to learn a bit about their work. Would you feel comfortable introducing us?

Keep it low-pressure and give them an easy way to decline.

If they agree, supply a short blurb Chris can use, making it easy for them:

Hi, Jordan! I want to introduce you to Taylor, a sharp early-career pro interested in what you do at [Company]. Taylor is proactive and genuinely curious about the field, and I thought you might have a good conversation!

Honestly, some of the best career moments sneak up on you when you least expect them. Maya joined an alumni book club mostly for the snacks and small talk, and somehow ended up meeting someone who ran events at a top creative firm. Raj just wanted to help out at a food bank, but wound up chatting with someone from his dream company. Even your online gaming buddies or that person you always see in a weirdly specific subreddit can turn out to be amazing contacts. People love helping out folks who share their interests, or at least their taste in memes.

Interactive Element: Network Mapping Exercise

Draw yourself at the center of a blank page. Radiate lines out to every contact you remember; think widely. Tag each by industry (tech, healthcare, nonprofit), influence (can hire/refer/recommend), and willingness to help (green = super helpful, yellow = maybe, red = rarely responds). Circle five "weak ties" you haven't connected with lately who are at interesting intersections (like an old teammate now in a field you're curious about). Pick one this week and send them a friendly catch-up email or text, just to say hi and share your latest.

The magic here? No awkward schmoozing or pretending to be someone you're not. You're simply spotting possibilities in the world you already live in and giving yourself a little nudge to reach out, even if it feels a bit cringey at first. Most people like helping out, as long as you're clear about what you're hoping to learn or do. And, honestly, the best connections usually come from the people you'd never expect.

LinkedIn, Slack, and Digital Networking Best Practices

LinkedIn is basically the main street of professional life, whether you love scrolling or you roll your eyes at every "thought leader" post. But giving your profile a little TLC can open doors. Start with your headline. Skip the boring "Marketing Associate" and get specific: "Digital Marketer | Growth Campaigns | B2B SaaS Storyteller." That way, recruiters know what you actually do and what makes you stand out. The "About" section? It's not your autobiography. Think of it like a movie trailer: Start with what gets you out of bed ("I help brands grow through data-driven storytelling"), toss in a big win ("Increased engagement by 40% at [Company]"), and wrap up with a call to action ("Let's connect if you love bold ideas and good coffee"). Keywords matter, too. Scan job posts for things like "SEO," "content strategy," or "project management," and work those in naturally. Don't just copy-paste a skills list; sneak those words into your story. If you're stuck, check out this before-and-after:

Before: "Recent graduate seeking opportunity in business."

After: "Analytical business grad with internship experience in e-commerce analytics, CRM optimization, and customer journey mapping. Looking to join a growth-minded team where data meets creative strategy."

See the difference? The second version gives recruiters something to latch onto, so you're not just another face in the crowd.

When it comes to LinkedIn, resist the urge to send out connection requests like you're trying to catch every Pokémon. Make each invite personal. Mention something you admire or a shared interest. For example: "Hi, Steve! I saw your post about product-led growth at [Company]. I'm working on those skills, too, and would love to connect." If you have a mutual contact, drop their name: "Hi, Wendy! [Mutual Contact] said we should connect, as apparently we're both into UX design." Skip the default message; those get ignored faster than gym promo emails. And once you're connected, don't go straight for the pitch. Start with a thank you, ask a real question, or comment on something they've posted recently.

Slack is its own weird little universe, part office banter, part project chat, part digital watercooler. In those big public channels, try being helpful before you start talking about yourself. Answer questions, share a resource, or point someone to a cool article. When you introduce yourself in a new channel, keep it short but memorable: "Hey, everyone! I'm Sam, obsessed with product design and weird ice cream flavors." If you want to start a conversation, jump into an existing thread with your two cents or ask a question that actually relates to your field ("Anyone else noticing trends in remote onboarding lately?"). That way, you're not shouting into the void.

Digital networking isn't about shouting your achievements from the rooftops. It's about showing up and being useful. Instead of just liking someone's post, leave a real comment. If someone shares an article on marketing trends, don't just type "Great post!" Add your own take: "Loved this! I've seen the same thing with B2B clients, especially when it comes to video content." Another easy win is to share articles or tools you think your network will actually use, and add a quick note like, "Saw this study on remote team productivity and figured it might help anyone prepping for hybrid work." That's how you become the person people turn to for good stuff, not just another self-promo machine.

Keeping Track and Staying on the Radar

One-off chats are fine, but the real magic happens when you stay on people's radar over time. Try setting up a super simple follow-up tracker in Google Sheets or Notion. Make columns for name, how you know them ("met via Product Hunt Slack"), the last time you talked, and what you want to do next ("share case study next month"). Every week or two, skim your list and send a quick note: "Saw this article and thought of you," or "Congrats on the product launch!" It takes almost no time, but it keeps things moving. No need for long essays; a line or two shows you care and keeps the connection alive.

Consistency wins over going all-in for a week and then ghosting everyone. You don't have to be everywhere or do everything; just show up in ways that feel like you. If you'd rather be online than at awkward mixers, own it. Digital networking is all about building tiny moments of trust that add up and sometimes open doors when you're not even looking.

Informational Interviews: Scripts, Questions, and Follow-Up

If the thought of forced elevator pitches and awkward networking events makes you want to run for the hills, you're not alone. That's where informational interviews come in; they're basically the introvert's secret weapon. Instead of being grilled under a spotlight, you get to steer the conversation, ask your own questions, and find out what a job or industry is really like. No pressure to perform or impress; it's a chance to get the inside scoop from someone who's been there.

Here's how the two differ:

Informational Interview vs Job Interview

	Informational Interview	Job Interview
Who's in Control?	You (the question-asker)	Employer (the evaluator)
Stakes	Low (no job on the line)	High (you're being assessed)
Main Goal	Learn, explore, connect	Get hired
Dress Code	Business casual / "Zoom chic"	Usually more formal
Who Initiates?	You (the question-asker)	Employer (the evaluator)

To request an informational interview, keep your outreach simple and authentic. Personalize your notes, whether by email or DM. For example:

Hi [Name], I've been following your work in [industry/company/project], and I'm curious about your journey in [field]. Would you be open to a quick coffee chat or call? I would appreciate your perspective, but no worries if timing isn't right.

For LinkedIn, keep it even shorter:

Hi [Name], I admire your work in [role/industry]. Could you spare 20 minutes for a quick call? I'm exploring similar paths and would love your insight.

If you share a mutual connection, mention it:

Hi [Mutual Contact], I noticed you know [Name] at [Company]. Would you be open to introducing us for a quick chat about their experience in [field]?

Once someone agrees to meet, show you're prepared by asking thoughtful, specific questions, not the ones easily Googled. Adapt your questions to your goals:

- **For career switchers:** "What's one myth about this field?" or "If you could start over, would you do anything differently?"
- **If eyeing internal moves:** "Which skills stand out at your company now?" or "How did you position yourself for advancement?"
- **Breaking into new industries:** "What surprised you most starting here?" and "How did you land your first role in this field?"
- **Basics:** "What does a typical day look like?" and "Are there resources or communities you recommend?"

Don't go in with a laundry list. Pick a few good questions so the conversation can actually flow.

The chat is just the start; effective follow-up is key. Send a personalized thank-you note within 24 hours:

Thank you again for sharing your experience at [Company], especially your advice about building cross-functional skills. It was really useful.

A quick thank you isn't just polite; it helps you stand out from the crowd.

If they recommended a resource, use it, then follow up within a week:

I read the article you suggested on [topic], and it really was insightful. Thanks again!

If you do try out their advice ("I joined that Slack group for marketers, and I'm already learning a ton!"), let them know. It shows you appreciate their help and that you're not just collecting tips for fun.

To keep things from going cold, set a reminder to check in every month or two. Send a quick article, say congrats on a new job, or share a tiny update ("I switched to UX design, your encouragement really helped!"). The goal is to add a little value and stay in touch, not to flood their inbox with updates.

A handy thank you template:

Hi [Name], I really appreciate you taking the time to chat about your career and insights into [industry/role]. Your suggestion about [specific tip] was especially helpful. I'm looking forward to putting it into action. Please let me know if I can ever return the favor!

When you do them right, informational interviews give you the real scoop on jobs and industries, and help you build relationships that might open doors later. You don't need to be super outgoing or have a million connections; be sure to ask good questions, listen, and then follow up. That's what sticks with people.

Think of informational interviews as research, not auditions.

Networking Up: Finding Mentors and Sponsor Relationships

You've probably heard people talk about "finding a mentor" or "getting a sponsor," but what do those roles look like in real life? They're not the same thing; each one helps you in a different way. Mentors are like your career GPS: They give advice, share their stories, help you through tough calls, and boost your confidence. You can ask them anything without feeling judged. Sponsors, on the other hand, are your behind-the-scenes hype squad. They use their influence to recommend you for jobs, promotions, or those meetings you didn't even know existed. Basically, mentors help you grow, whereas sponsors help you get in the room.

Think of it like a two-by-two grid: Mentors give you guidance and feedback; sponsors give you a boost and open doors. You need both. If you only have one, you might miss out on some pretty important opportunities.

If you want to find a mentor or sponsor without coming off as too transactional, skip the awkward "Will you be my mentor?" email. Instead, show real interest in what they do, leave a thoughtful comment on their LinkedIn post, show up to their webinar, or ask a good question during a Q&A. A simple message like "I caught your panel on remote leadership and really liked your take on junior staff visibility. Mind if I ask a follow-up?" is a great way to start. If you want to meet, keep it straightforward but chill: "Hi, [Name], I'm inspired by your work in [field]. I'm early in my career and would love to learn about [specific area]. Any chance you'd be up for a quick coffee or Zoom? I can totally work around your schedule."

Once you land a meeting, show up ready and don't waste their time. Start with a thank you, share why you reached out ("I'd love to hear more about [topic] and your story"), and ask for advice that's tied to their experience. Keep it focused: "I'd love to know how you made early career pivots and what you look for in people you support." And don't forget to share your own goals; mentorship works best when your mentor knows what you're aiming for.

To keep these connections going, set expectations early. Ask how they like to stay in touch: monthly emails, quarterly check-ins, or the occasional text. Respect their boundaries and don't push for more than they offer. Always send a thank you note and let them know how you used their advice: "I tried your tip about leading team standups and got great feedback. Thanks again!" That way, you keep the relationship alive and show you're serious.

Watch out for the classic mistakes, such as treating mentors like advice vending machines and then ghosting them after you get what you want. Don't make every chat all about you. Mentors are busy, so respect their time and try to give back, even if it's just sharing a cool article or inviting them to something interesting.

Consider Paula, who checked in quarterly with her mentor, not just with requests but also to share progress and express gratitude. When a director role opened, the mentor recommended her because Paula had proven her dedication and reliability. In contrast, Carl lost contact after only reaching out when he needed help and never following up, so his mentor became distant.

Sponsors are an even bigger deal; they're putting their own reputation out there for you. If someone's willing to go to bat for you, keep them in the loop on your wins and always follow through. Nobody wants to stick their neck out for someone who flakes.

Building these relationships takes time and a little realness. Don't try to force it. Just show up, stay curious, follow through, and be yourself. Mentors help you grow, and sponsors help you move up. Both are worth having in your corner for the long haul.

Networking for Introverts: Quiet Influence and Sustainable Outreach

There's this myth that networking is only for people who love working a room, shaking 20 hands before lunch, and telling stories that start with, "You'll never guess who I met." But, honestly, introverts have some of the best networking superpowers, like truly listening, asking good questions, and making people feel heard. Sure, extroverts might rack up more business cards, but introverts often build stronger connections because they care more about quality than quantity. In one-on-one conversations or small groups, that quiet depth becomes a real advantage. They're not trying to dominate the room so much as make real connections, remember the details, and skip the endless small talk that leaves everyone drained.

If the idea of walking into a ballroom full of strangers makes you want to suddenly remember a dentist appointment, you're definitely not alone. The good news is that there are plenty of ways to grow your network without pretending to be someone you're not. Small group meetups, like book clubs, industry breakfasts, or hobby groups, are much less intimidating and often lead to real conversations. Online spaces like Discord or niche Slack channels are introvert goldmines; you get time to think before you reply and can join in at your own pace. And don't underestimate the power of a simple coffee chat; invite one person for a low-key conversation (virtual or in-person). No pressure, just a chance to talk shop, swap advice, or share stories about the weirdest office parties you've encountered.

When you do have to show up at a networking event or mixer, prep is your best friend. Come up with a quick, real intro for yourself, something like, "I'm Erin, and I help healthcare teams use data to improve patient care." Practice it until it doesn't sound weird coming out of your mouth. Before you go, pick one or two topics you'd actually enjoy talking about (maybe your latest project or a cool article you read), and think of a question to ask others ("What's the most interesting thing you've worked on lately?"). If social stuff drains you fast, plan your escape ahead of time. Maybe you only stay for 45 minutes, or have a friend text you at a set time, like when you're trying to get out of a bad first date. And after, give yourself a little reward: Take a walk, listen to music, or just sit in silence for a bit. That way, networking doesn't turn into instant burnout.

Staying in touch doesn't mean you have to be glued to your inbox, firing off memes and motivational quotes every week. Sustainable networking is about being consistent without burning yourself out.

Try batch networking: Pick one day a month to catch up, send a few messages, schedule a coffee chat, or just scroll through LinkedIn updates in one go. That way, you're not stressing about constant outreach, but you're still on people's radar when something comes up. When you do reach out, use a simple template to keep it easy but personal. Shoot a quick note for someone's work anniversary ("Congrats on three years at [Company]! Hope you're celebrating with good coffee!") or when they launch a new project ("Saw your launch, and it looks awesome!"). These little check-ins don't have to be long, but they show you're paying attention.

Low-key outreach can be as easy as sending a happy birthday text, congratulating someone on a promotion, or leaving a thoughtful comment on their latest post. If you want to get fancy, set reminders for these dates in your phone or a simple spreadsheet so nobody falls off your radar. The trick is to make each message count; a few well-timed notes do more for your reputation than daily check-ins ever could.

Networking doesn't have to be a full-time job or something only extroverts are good at. It's about finding what works for you, using your listening skills, going for real connections over simply collecting contacts, and building habits that keep relationships alive without zapping all your energy. The quiet influence introverts bring is seriously underrated. Sustainable outreach keeps you connected and visible but still lets you be yourself.

As you finish up this chapter, remember: Your voice matters just as much as anyone else's in the networking world, even if it's on the quieter side. Up next, you'll see how all these connections can open doors for new skills, growth, and a career path built on real relationships, not just a bunch of clever handshakes.

Chapter 6

Career Moves and Smart Decision-Making

Breaking Out of a Plateau: Signals It's Time for Your Next Move

Let's say you're in yet another meeting, pretending to care about spreadsheet formatting, secretly Googling "how to know if you're stuck at work." Maybe your boss keeps telling you to "keep up the great work," but you haven't learned anything new since your last TV binge. If you're constantly restless or disengaged, you might be on a career plateau, a subtle stall that can hit at any stage.

Career plateaus are sneaky. One day, you're cruising along, thinking you're making progress, and then you look up and realize you haven't moved in months. The warning signs? They're everywhere once you know what to look for. If you're bored out of your mind by lunchtime, and every task feels like you've done it a hundred times before, that's a big clue. Or maybe you haven't learned anything new since your first week, and the only training you've seen lately is figuring out how to fix the coffee machine. Feeling invisible is another classic, like when you get passed over for projects, your reviews sound like they were copied and pasted, or your job feels like a never-ending loop of the same old stuff. If nobody's even mentioned your growth or next steps in ages, you're not just in a slow patch. You're officially stuck.

But not every slow week means you're stuck forever. There's a big difference between a little downtime and the kind of stuck that makes you want to Google "how to escape my job" at 2 a.m. So, how long have you felt this way? A couple of quiet weeks? Totally normal. But if you've been in the same rut for six months (or longer) with zero new challenges, it's probably not just a phase. Sometimes it's the job, no room to grow, a boss who micromanages every move, or an industry that's shrinking faster than your favorite sweater in the wash. Other times, it's you, maybe you stopped raising your hand for new opportunities or forgot to ask for feedback. Before you make any big moves, take a minute to figure out what's really going on.

Interactive Element: "Stay, Grow, or Go?" Assessment

Rate from 1 (not me) to 5 (100% me):

Stay, Grow, or Go? Scorecard

	1	2	3	4	5
I'm bored most days and rarely learn.	○	○	○	○	○
My tasks are so repetitive that I could do them in my sleep.	○	○	○	○	○
No one's discussed my career development in months.	○	○	○	○	○
I feel invisible for stretch assignments.	○	○	○	○	○
I daydream about leaving or switching fields at least weekly.	○	○	○	○	○
My performance reviews never mention a growth plan.	○	○	○	○	○
I haven't added or used new skills in over six months.	○	○	○	○	○
Total Score:					

Over 20? It's time to get serious about your next move.

Before you go full rage-quit or change your LinkedIn to "Open to Anything," hit pause. Is it really the job that's stuck, or have you just gotten a little too comfy in your routine? Sometimes the problem is outside your control, like a team so small you can't move, a boss who keeps all the good stuff for themselves, or an industry that's slowly fading away. But sometimes, it's on you; maybe you've settled in because the paycheck is steady, or you're letting imposter syndrome keep you from trying something new.

Try a self-inventory:

- Do your values still match your company's?
- Are there projects or teams at work for which you could learn or stretch?
- What would make you excited about work again: more responsibility, new skills, or a new mission?
- Are you seeking purpose, or just wanting out?

If you crave challenge but nothing around fits, it might be time for a new environment. But if opportunities exist and you haven't stepped up, sometimes one game-changing conversation or new initiative can break the cycle.

People break plateaus all the time, sometimes with bold leaps and sometimes by reframing what's already there. Donna, a midlevel marketer, realized she hadn't learned anything new in two years. Tired of copy-paste reviews, she started shadowing the product management team and picked up skills that earned her a career shift and more opportunities. Lena, working at a grant-frozen nonprofit with stalled projects, started a podcast on social impact after hours. It built her network and led to consulting gigs.

If you're reading these stories and thinking, *That's not me (yet)*, don't panic. Start small. Even trading one boring task for something new or pitching a project you actually care about can shake things up. But if you've checked every single plateau box and nothing changes, even after you've tried, maybe it's time to take the hint. There are more paths out there than you can see from where you're sitting. Sometimes breaking out means making your own path from scratch.

The Career Pivot Playbook: Switching Industries or Roles Step-by-Step

Changing your job is one thing; swapping industries or roles is a whole different beast. If a job search is like moving to a new apartment in your neighborhood, a pivot is moving across town and learning all the shortcuts from scratch. It's not just a matter of updating your résumé and hoping for a slightly better desk. Instead, a pivot reboots what you do, who you work with, and how you talk about yourself. Let's break it down: A **"pivot"** moves you into a new lane (different work, fresh field), while a **"transition"** often means a new company but the same skills, and a **"promotion"** is just climbing higher where you already stand. Here's the cheat sheet:

Promotion vs Transition vs Pivot

Path	What Changes?	Risk Level	Primary Reward
Promotion	Title, scope, responsibility	Low	Higher pay & status
Transition	Company or team	Medium	New environment & skills
Pivot	Role or industry	High	New path & growth

So, how do you pull off a pivot without feeling like an imposter in every meeting? Start with brutal self-assessment. What skills do you bring that matter in your new field? List every project, tool, and success, even if it feels random. Ask yourself which of these can solve problems in the role you want. Transferable skills are your currency, things like project management, data analysis, customer relations, or creativity. Don't just guess; compare job postings in your target field and highlight the overlaps with what you already know.

Next, dig into research mode. Find out what's hot (and what's not) in your desired industry. Read blogs, follow insiders on LinkedIn, and stalk company career pages. Pinpoint the skills that keep showing up; these are your new "must-haves." Now comes the gap analysis: Mark which ones you already have and which are missing. If you spot holes, fill them as quickly as possible. Start an online course, volunteer for a side project, or build a mini-portfolio, even if it's just one killer case study.

Rebranding yourself is critical, and it starts with language. Rewrite your résumé and LinkedIn so every bullet speaks your target industry's dialect. For example, if you're moving from sales to marketing, swap "closed deals" for "drove campaigns that increased engagement." Your new headline should scream where you're headed, not where you've been: "Analytical problem-solver pivoting to digital marketing" beats "Experienced account executive." Use n-grams (common word combinations that frequently appear together, like "project management" or "data analysis") and lemmatization (slightly adjusting words to match how employers phrase them, like using "analyze" instead of "analyzing") to your advantage; scan job ads for repeating verbs and sprinkle them naturally into your profile.

Résumé "Secret Sauce": Speak the Employer's Language

Most job descriptions aren't as unique as they look. When you read several postings for the same role, you'll start noticing the same words and phrases showing up again and again. That repetition is not an accident; it's a signal.

Recruiters and hiring systems scan for patterns. If your résumé uses a totally different vocabulary, even strong experience can get overlooked. The goal isn't to copy job descriptions word for word; it's to translate your experience into the language employers already recognize.

Use this quick checklist before you apply:

- Read 3–5 job postings for roles you want.
- Highlight verbs and phrases that repeat ("own," "analyze," "collaborate," "optimize," "lead").
- Circle skills that appear across multiple listings.
- Rewrite your bullets using that language, naturally.
- Double-check that everything still sounds like *you*.

For example, if multiple postings mention "cross-functional collaboration," don't just list tasks. Show how you partnered with other teams to deliver results. Same work, clearer signal.

This was a turning point for me. Once I realized how often employers reuse the same language and started adjusting my résumé accordingly, I began getting more interviews without changing my actual experience. Nothing about my background suddenly improved, only how clearly it matched what employers were already looking for.

This isn't keyword stuffing or gaming the system. It's alignment. When your résumé mirrors the language of the role, your experience feels natural instead of forced. That small shift can be the difference between getting skimmed and getting called.

Next Step: Activating Your Pivot Strategy

Networking is the secret passage most people ignore. Reach out to folks already doing what you want to do. Ask smart questions ("What surprised you most about moving into this field?"). Use your "pivot pitch," a short story connecting your past wins to future goals. Try something like "I've spent three years optimizing client experiences in hospitality, and now I'm eager to bring that same focus to customer success in tech." Don't just talk; listen for advice and offer help where you can.

When applying, customize every application. This step matters more than most people realize, and it played a big role in my own job searches. Ditch the generic cover letter and instead link specific past achievements to problems you'll solve in the new role. Build a small but mighty portfolio, even if it's just one relevant project or a thoughtful mockup, that lets hiring managers actually see you in action. If you're moving into design from education, redesign a classroom resource as a portfolio piece.

To keep this from feeling overwhelming, use a 90-day pivot plan. Break it into weeks: weeks 1–2 for research and skills audit; weeks 3–6 for upskilling and rebranding; weeks 7–10 for networking and building your pivot pitch; and weeks 11–12 for targeted applications and interviews. Each week, set one or two specific goals (e.g., "Connect with three people in my target field," "Finish one short course," "Rewrite LinkedIn headline"). Track progress in a spreadsheet. Notion or Google Sheets works great, so nothing gets lost in the shuffle.

Celebrate milestones along the way. Landed an info interview? Treat yourself to your favorite coffee. Published your first cross-industry project? Brag to a friend or post it on LinkedIn. Small wins deserve real celebration; they build momentum when doubts creep in.

Here's your Pivot Action Plan template:

Pivot Action Plan

- **Weeks 1–2:** Self-assessment and skills mapping
- **Weeks 3–6:** Gap analysis and micro-upskilling
- **Weeks 7–10:** Rebranding and networking
- **Weeks 11–12:** Targeted applications
- **Ongoing:** Track wins and celebrate progress

Pivoting doesn't mean you need to find another job; it means you're building a new story for yourself, one step at a time. The best part? You get to keep all your old skills and add new ones, making you both unique and resilient wherever your career takes you next.

Weighing Multiple Job Offers: Decision Matrices and Checklists

So, you finally did it. After all the interviews, awkward video calls, and "Tell me about a time when..." questions, you find yourself in a rare but stressful spot: more than one job offer on the table. You should feel like a rockstar, but honestly, you're probably just overwhelmed. Which one do you pick? Do you go with the shinier title or with the company that offers snacks and remote Fridays? This is where most people start listening to everyone else's opinions: parents, friends, and that random coworker who's never actually switched jobs. Instead of flipping a coin or crowdsourcing your future, try using a decision matrix. This tool is like the adult version of a pro/con list, but less likely to leave you awake at 2 a.m. second-guessing yourself.

Start by making a simple table. Down the left, list your categories: "salary," "health benefits," "flexibility," "growth opportunities," "company mission," "manager chemistry," "promotion track," "team culture," "remote options," whatever matters most. Across the top, put "Offer A" and "Offer B" (or C, if you're living the dream). Now, rate each category for every offer on a scale from 1 (bleh) to 5 (amazing). Let's say Offer A gives you more cash but zero flexibility, while Offer B matches your values and lets you work in sweats. Suddenly, it's not just about numbers.

But don't stop at numbers. Not all categories matter equally. Maybe health insurance is a dealbreaker for you, or perhaps the option to work from Bali tips the scale. Assign weights to each category; maybe "growth" gets a 3x multiplier while "cool office art" gets a 1. Multiply each score by its weight, add up the totals for each offer, and there's your data-driven winner (or at least a way to see what's really important for you). You can find templates online or build one in Google Sheets. Treat this as your personal "reduce regret" machine.

Here's how it can look:

Decision Matrix

Category	Weight (x)	Offer A	Offer B
Base Salary	2	4	3
Benefits	3	2	3
Flexibility	3	1	5
Team Culture	1	4	2
Growth Path	3	3	4
Total		**30**	**44**

Total it up. The higher score usually reveals which job suits your life right now, not just which is shinier on LinkedIn.

I wish I had used a decision matrix the one time I had two offers on the table. I relied on my gut and overlooked a few things that mattered more than I realized. Looking back, writing it all out might have saved me months of regret. That experience is why I swear by this tool now; it helps you make a choice you can stand behind.

How to Negotiate

Now, let's talk about negotiating while you're still deciding. Employers expect some careful thinking (unless they're offering you your dream gig and want an answer before you even leave the Zoom call). Don't be afraid to ask for more time, especially if offers overlap or something feels unclear. You can say, "Thank you so much for the offer. I'm excited about the possibility! Could I have until Friday to review everything and get back to you?" That sounds respectful and confident. If they press for an answer sooner than feels right, try "I want to make sure I can consider this thoroughly. Would a few extra days be possible?" Most companies will give you at least a little breathing room.

If you need more info, ask directly. Email works well: "Could you clarify how bonuses are calculated?" or "Would it be possible to see a sample benefits guide?" It's not pushy; it's responsible. In fact, this signals to employers that you make decisions based on facts, not FOMO.

Negotiation doesn't end just because the initial offer has landed. If you lean toward one job but wish it checked another box (say, remote days or signing bonus), speak up before signing anything: "I'm very interested in moving forward. Is there any flexibility on remote workdays or professional development support?" You might get more than you expect just by asking.

Every decision comes with its own flavor of what-ifs. I've seen software engineers walk away from huge salaries at big firms in favor of tiny startups. One friend did this for growth and ended up running his own team within two years. He said the chaos was real, but the learning curve was worth every late night. On the flip side, I know nonprofit pros who picked mission over money and felt proud, but later struggled with burnout when raises never materialized. Both types learned lessons only experience can teach: Sometimes you win big; other times, you learn what truly matters for your next move.

The best thing about using a system like this? It slices right through all the noise and shiny distractions. No more picking jobs based on a gut feeling or getting lured in by perks you'll forget about by week three. Take a breath, pull up your spreadsheet or checklist, and put what matters to you front and center before you make any move that messes with your paycheck or your sanity.

Lateral Moves, Side Hustles, and Portfolio Careers Explained

Careers today are more like a buffet than a fixed menu; you're not limited to one choice. Climbing the corporate ladder is just one route; sometimes, moving sideways or even stepping outdoors is the smart play. In a traditional career, you move up in the same department (assistant to manager to director). A lateral move means shifting to a new function at the same level, while portfolio careers mix multiple gigs, freelance work, side hustles, and sometimes part-time jobs. Each path has pros and cons, so understanding them helps you match your risk, learning, and lifestyle appetite.

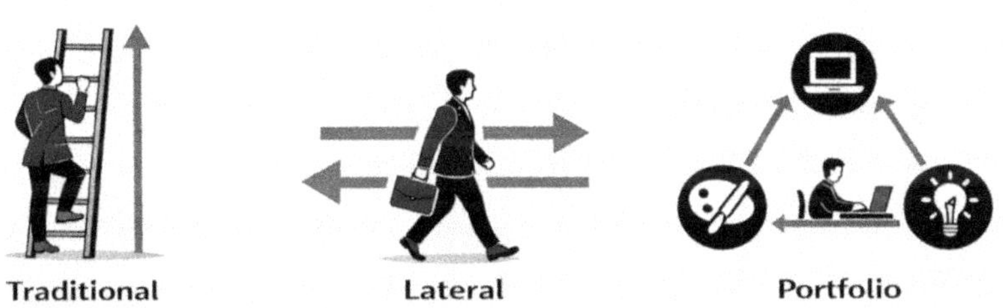

Path	Main Feature	Risk	Reward
Traditional	Vertical promotions	Low	Predictable
Lateral	Same level, new function	Medium	Broader skills
Portfolio	Multiple gigs/roles	High	Flexibility

Lateral moves address the feeling of burnout or boredom, letting you try new roles without switching companies. Maybe you're in operations but want a taste of project management, or you're moving from sales to customer success. These transitions might not immediately increase your pay, but they can teach you new skills, expose you to fresh perspectives, and expand your internal network. For example, someone switching from finance to HR might not receive a higher title, but they can master company-wide lingo and become the go-to for cross-team communication. Participating in cross-functional projects or switching departments helps break monotony and boost your long-term value.

If you fantasize about earning extra cash or exploring creative outlets beyond your main job, side hustles are ideal. They range from freelance writing to tutoring or building websites for local shops, whatever excites you and brings in extra income. Before diving in, check your company's "no moonlighting" or conflict-of-interest policies and be honest about your available time and energy. Prioritize your main job to avoid issues, and be realistic: Side hustles are still work.

Side Hustle Readiness Checklist

- Do you have at least five hours a week free?
- Is your employer okay with side gigs?
- Can you keep jobs separate?
- Are you ready to handle taxes and invoices?
- What does success look like (more money, clients, skills, or just fun)?

Track everything: Use a basic spreadsheet for hours, tasks, income, and skills developed. For example, a marketing analyst who moonlights as a social media manager should log each campaign and result. This builds confidence and proof of skill for future opportunities.

Portfolio careers take things further: When one side hustle isn't enough, or when you want work/life control, you juggle several gigs, maybe consulting, teaching, contract work, writing, and more. This requires managing multiple clients, invoices, deadlines, and communication styles (from emoji-loving to formal types). But it offers flexibility: Pick projects you like and pass on those you don't.

Example: Monday and Tuesday for a client's design work, Wednesday morning teaching online, Thursday afternoon copywriting for a nonprofit, and Friday reserved for your personal project. The variety is the advantage; you set your own mix and can adjust as interests shift. Many creative professionals balance consulting, teaching, and publishing while keeping schedules open for unexpected opportunities.

Tips for Portfolio Careers

- Develop strong time management and set boundaries.
- Use tools like calendars and project trackers.
- Set clear goals for each gig (money, experience, networking).
- Review monthly to keep the best gigs, and drop the rest.

The gig economy isn't just for drivers or coders; it's open to anyone craving autonomy or variety beyond traditional roles. The challenge is balancing freedom with security, so maintain an emergency fund and a backup plan.

Communicating Your Career Change: Storytelling for New Opportunities

When you're shaking up your career, the scariest part isn't the job search; it's explaining yourself. Suddenly, every chat, interview, or DM feels like you're auditioning for a role in your own life story. And honestly, nobody wants to sound lost or apologetic when they talk about a big leap. Here's where storytelling saves the day. The "Before, During, After" framework works wonders. Start with where you've been (Before), walk through the realization or trigger that made you rethink things (During), then finish with where you're going and why it's a logical next step (After). For example: "I spent years teaching, and while I loved helping students, I realized my favorite part was designing creative ways to solve tricky problems. That led me to product design, where I can channel those skills into building tools for others."

The trick is being clear and confident; no one wants to hear a rambling apology for not knowing what they want to be when they grow up. When someone asks, "Why are you making this change?" borrow this plug-and-play script: "I've achieved a lot in [old field], but over time, I found myself drawn to [new field] because it lets me use my strengths in [key skill] and make a bigger impact." For networking, keep it short and punchy: "I'm shifting from [old job] to [new field] because I've realized that's where my skills and interests intersect." An elevator pitch for career changers can sound like, "With a background in [first field] and a passion for [core skill], I'm excited to bring a fresh perspective and energy to [target industry]."

Make Sure Everything Is Updated

Updating your written materials is just as important as nailing your spoken story. Your résumé headline should look forward, not backward. Instead of "Experienced Retail Associate," try "Customer Experience Specialist Pivoting to SaaS Support." The LinkedIn "About" section is where you can really weave your Before-During-After story into a single, compelling narrative. Here's a formula: Start with your old expertise, mention the moment you noticed a pattern or spark ("I noticed I was most energized when..."), and close with how these strengths are the perfect fit for your new direction ("I'm now applying this skillset to..."). This approach transforms your profile from a list of unrelated jobs into a cohesive story that makes recruiters nod rather than scratch their heads.

Addressing gaps, wild cards, or even setbacks? You don't have to hide them. Instead, frame them as growth moments. If you took a sabbatical or got laid off, use something like: "After leaving my last role, I took time to [learn/volunteer/care for family], which helped clarify my strengths and priorities." If a side project didn't pan out, try: "Launching my own freelance project taught me resilience and gave me hands-on experience with [skill], even though it didn't become a full-time gig." Real confidence comes from owning your choices, even the weird ones. Employers appreciate honesty and guts more than a spotless but boring record.

Failure happens; what matters is what you learned. Imagine someone who went all-in on a startup that fizzled after a year. Instead of brushing it under the rug, they might say, "Launching my own business taught me how to build partnerships from scratch. While it didn't scale as planned, I gained firsthand experience in client management, pitching ideas, and learning on my feet." That's not failure; it's proof they tried things, adapted quickly, and brought hard-earned lessons to the table. When you control the narrative, even detours become assets.

The whole point is making your career change feel like the most natural progression in the world, even if it's anything but. People want to understand your logic. They want to see that you're not running away from something, but running toward something better. Use your story everywhere: in interviews, on LinkedIn, in casual networking chats, or even when updating your email signature if you're feeling bold. Consistency is key; if your story stays true across platforms and conversations, you'll start believing it yourself, and so will everyone else. That's often the moment when your career stops feeling uncertain and starts gaining real momentum.

Remember that every move, big or small, gets easier when you tell your story with clarity and confidence. A strong narrative doesn't just open doors; it builds trust and excitement around where you're heading next. In the next chapter, we'll tackle how to keep your momentum going once you've landed that new opportunity, without falling back into old habits or endless hustle.

Chapter 7

Building an Authentic Personal Brand

Creating Your Personal Brand Statement: Standing Out Authentically

Imagine walking into a room where everyone seems to have their signature move: the designer rocking neon sneakers, the project manager who always has snacks, the developer who can fix anything except their own sleep schedule. And there you are, wondering, *Wait, what's my thing? Am I just another square in the Zoom grid?* Here's the secret: You already have a brand, even if you've never thought about it. It's not some fancy logo or a cheesy marketing slogan. It's the mix of your quirks, your values, your strengths, and the way you make people feel. The real challenge is figuring out what makes you stick in people's minds on purpose, and not just because you once dumped coffee on your boss's laptop.

Here's a way to start that's less cringey than your last team icebreaker. Ask yourself what people thank you for. Not just the big, heroic stuff like "saving the day" or "fixing the printer when it was making that weird noise," but the little things, like listening without judging, making sense of confusing instructions, turning a spreadsheet from a headache into something readable, or staying calm when everyone else is losing it. Still drawing a blank? Text three friends or coworkers and ask them, "Hey, random question: What's something you think I'm really good at?" The answers might surprise you. Maybe it's something you've heard a million times and shrugged off, or maybe it's brand new, like "You always crack a joke when things get tense" or "You're the only one who can explain our benefits package in a way that doesn't make my brain melt."

Look for the stuff that keeps coming up. Scroll through your old thank-you notes, Slack messages, or group chats and see what people have said about you. Are you always the one explaining things? The person who connects everyone? The calm one when things go sideways? The creative problem-solver? These are gold. Your strengths don't have to look like anyone else's; in fact, it's better if they don't.

Now, try to squish all that good stuff into a personal brand statement. Skip the corporate buzzwords; nobody needs to hear you're a "dynamic go-getter" or a "results-oriented team player." Instead, use this super-simple formula:

Personal Brand Statement

I help [*audience*]
achieve [*result*]
by leveraging [*unique strengths*].

- Clear
- Specific
- Sounds like you
- No buzzwords

This keeps it real and specific. Here are a few examples:

- **Tech:** "I help startups squash bugs and launch faster by translating code into plain English for non–tech teams."
- **Nonprofit:** "I help mission-driven orgs rally supporters by combining creative storytelling with ruthless project organization."
- **Creative:** "I help small brands stand out online by turning ideas into scroll-stopping visuals and campaigns."

Each one is specific, easy to understand, and communicates real impact, not just aspirations.

Take a moment to write your own. Even a rough first draft works:

- "I help new team members feel at home by sharing knowledge and checking in regularly."
- "I help chaotic projects hit deadlines by breaking down big goals into doable steps, and making sure everyone laughs at least once."

Don't make it harder than it needs to be. You're not writing your life story, just trying to catch the main vibe of how you help people, over and over.

Interactive Element: Brand Statement Stress Test

Jot down three versions of your statement. Then, give each one a quick reality check: Would a total stranger get what you mean? Send your favorite to a friend or coworker and ask, "Does this sound like me?" If it feels weird or fake, tweak it until it feels right. You want to end up with something short, memorable, and real that you wouldn't cringe saying out loud.

Before finalizing, do this authenticity check:

- Does it sound like something you would actually say?
- Would your friends agree, without laughing or rolling their eyes?
- Does it avoid vague, generic buzzwords like "synergy" or "rockstar"?
- Is it clear who you help and how?
- Could you put it in your email signature or say it out loud comfortably?

If you catch yourself slipping into corporate-speak, like "leveraging cross-functional synergies for scalable growth," stop and swap it for something real, like "I help teams talk to each other so projects actually get finished." Real-life examples always win over empty buzzwords.

Try your statement out on someone who has no idea what you do, such as a roommate or a friend from a totally different department. If they get it right away, you're good. If they look confused, make it simpler. Clear always wins over clever.

Once you know what makes you stand out and you say it in your own way, introductions get much less awkward. You'll stick in people's minds without having to try too hard or fake it.

LinkedIn Profiles That Get Noticed (Without the Cringe)

If your LinkedIn profile is collecting digital dust or just looks like you copy-pasted your résumé into a website, you're missing out. Recruiters, future teammates, and even that person you met at a conference are probably checking you out before you ever say hi. They want to know what you're about, your skills, your story, and your vibe, not just a list of "corporate robot greatest hits." Let's make your profile something people remember, so they want to connect (or at least ask for your Netflix recommendations).

Start with your headline. This is not the spot for "Seeking Opportunities" or "Results-Oriented Team Player"; those are as exciting as plain toast and about as useful. Instead, mix in the keywords people search for with a little bit of your personality. Think about what your work best friend would say you do: "Project Manager | Building Creative Teams & Turning Chaos Into Clarity" or "Data Analyst | Telling Stories With Numbers and Coffee." Use the words recruiters tend to look for (your job, your specialty, the usual buzzwords), but don't forget to sound like a real person. And please, don't try to cram in every buzzword you can think of; nobody's impressed by "Synergy Synergizer."

The "About" Is Your Movie Trailer

Now for the "About" section. This isn't just a place to dump your job history or copy-paste your cover letter with fancier words. Think of it like the trailer for your career movie, just enough to make people want to see the whole thing. Start with a line that sounds like you, not just your job title: "I get fired up helping nonprofits turn big ideas into campaigns that actually move people." Then, sneak in your personal brand statement from earlier. Don't just list what you do; talk about the impact you've had and why it matters to you. Finish with a hint about your values, what you're excited about, or where you want to go next.

Here's how a typical "About" might sound before using this approach:

I am a marketing professional with three years of experience in social media management, campaign execution, and analytics. Skilled in Facebook Ads, content creation, and Google Analytics. Looking for new opportunities in digital marketing.

And now, with a brand statement woven in:

Turning scrolls into clicks and clicks into real conversations is my favorite challenge. I help small brands break through the noise by mixing creative storytelling with data-driven experiments. Whether I'm launching a scrappy Instagram campaign or analyzing audience trends, I'm happiest when I'm building something that gets results and makes people smile. If your team loves big ideas (and good memes), let's chat.

Being credible doesn't mean you have to sound like a robot. Show some warmth by sharing endorsements or recommendations from people who actually know what you do. Go for folks who can tell a quick story about you, not just "Dale is a hard worker," but "Dale pulled off a product launch in two days when our vendor disappeared." Sprinkle in a little humor or something human if it fits: maybe your love for color-coded spreadsheets or your weird talent for finding the best lunch spots within five blocks of any office.

Don't forget about multimedia. LinkedIn lets you add videos, slide decks, project links, or articles right under each job or in the featured section. Throw in a short video intro (even if it's just you talking about why you love your work), screenshots from presentations, or links to blog posts you've written. This isn't just for designers; HR folks can show off onboarding guides, engineers can share GitHub projects, and marketers can link to campaign samples. Suddenly, your profile isn't just a list of claims; it's proof you've done some cool stuff.

Now, let's talk about the classic mistakes everyone makes at least once. If you over-polish, you sound fake. If you humble-brag, it's like you're trying to win a trophy that doesn't exist. If you're too generic, nobody remembers you after their coffee break. Watch out for these red flag phrases:

- "Results-oriented team player" → Swap for something like "I love building teams that turn big messes into tidy wins."
- "Detail-oriented professional" → Try "I spot typos on menus and fix broken processes before they become headaches."
- "Motivated self-starter" → Go for "I once automated my own onboarding checklist because I couldn't stand waiting for IT."

Every part of your profile should sound like you and show what makes you tick, not just what makes you hirable. Write like you're chatting with a curious neighbor or someone you'd actually want to work with, not auditioning for a reality show. If you keep it real and specific, you'll attract the right opportunities (and people) who want exactly what you bring, quirks included.

Building a Digital Portfolio: Demonstrating Projects, Skills, and Growth

A digital portfolio isn't just for designers or people who live in Photoshop. It's for anyone who wants to prove they can do more than what a résumé or LinkedIn profile shows. If you're in HR, a portfolio helps you stand out from the usual "people-person" crowd. Marketers can show off campaigns from a wild idea to launch. Tech folks can highlight side projects or automations that would otherwise get lost in the daily shuffle. A portfolio puts all your best stuff in one spot, so employers, clients, or future teammates can clearly see what you can do. This "show, don't just tell" move works for everyone: teachers, analysts, nonprofit folks, you name it.

The trick is to curate, not dump. Don't stuff your portfolio with every project you've ever touched; think highlight reel, not endless scroll. Focus on what made a difference: Did you save time, boost engagement, solve a real problem, or pick up a new skill? Go for quality, not just quantity. For each project, try the STAR method:

- **Situation:** What was happening?
- **Task:** What was your responsibility or goal?
- **Action:** What did you actually do?
- **Result:** What changed because of your work?

For example, don't just write, "Ran onboarding." Spell it out with STAR: "Situation: High turnover. Task: Redesign onboarding. Action: Built training modules and weekly check-ins. Result: Retention went up 30% in six months." This works whether you led a team, volunteered, or did a solo side project. Mix it up by adding solo work, group stuff, volunteer gigs, and side hustles. Before you add anything, ask yourself, *Did I learn or grow? Did I actually solve a problem? Would I talk about this in an interview? Does it show off a new skill or strength?*

Tools to Help You Build Your Portfolio

Building your portfolio doesn't have to be hard or cost a fortune. Tools like Notion, Google Sites, Wix, and Carrd are all easy to use and won't break the bank. Notion is great if you like things clean and simple. Google Sites is quick to set up and plays nicely with Google Docs. Wix has tons of templates if you want something polished. Carrd is perfect for a simple, mobile-friendly page you can make in an hour. Set up a clear homepage ("About Me"), a projects section (with your STAR stories), and a way for people to contact you. Organize by skills or topics that make sense for your work: "Campaigns," "Tech Projects," "Process Improvements," "Workshops," "Training Guides," and so on. Use screenshots and show before-and-after results, code snippets, campaign images, dashboards, or even nice feedback you've gotten.

Once your portfolio is ready, don't hide it. Put the link in your LinkedIn "Featured" section and in your contact info so people can find it. Add it to your email signature, something like, "See my latest work: [your link]" so every email is a little nudge. If you have a personal website or online résumé, stick the link there, too. Make sure it's easy to get around so that if someone clicks in from LinkedIn, they should land right on a project page that shows what you can do. For example, if your LinkedIn headline is about creative onboarding, your portfolio should show off your training materials and the story behind that 30% retention boost.

A digital portfolio is proof that you're growing and learning, not just repeating the same old tasks. HR folks can show off new policies or culture projects. Marketers can share analytics or campaign materials. Teachers might add lesson plans, student feedback, or creative projects. Tech people can include GitHub repos, dashboards, or app demos. The point isn't to win awards; it's to make your work and its impact clear. Keep your portfolio fresh with new wins or lessons learned. Think of it as your personal highlight reel, a place that shows how you solve problems and think things through. When someone asks what you bring to the table, just send them the link and let your work do the talking.

Thought Leadership for Beginners: Sharing Insights, Not Hype

Thought leadership sounds kind of scary, like you need a turtleneck, a podcast, and your own quotes on inspirational backgrounds. But honestly, it's much simpler (and much less cringey) in that you are simply sharing useful tips, honest lessons, and those "oh, wow, I wish I'd known that" moments you pick up along the way. You don't need ten years of experience, a book deal, or a viral TED Talk. What you do need is the guts to talk about what you're learning, failures and all, and share something real. Maybe your last project fell apart because everyone misunderstood the brief, or maybe you just found a shortcut in Excel that saved you an hour. Those are the nuggets that actually help people.

Take the young analyst who shared a post about botching their first big client presentation—slides out of order, nerves everywhere, the whole deal. Instead of hiding it, they wrote a short LinkedIn post titled "How I Bombed My First Client Call (And What I'll Do Differently Next Time)." It wasn't self-pity or chest-thumping; they just told the story, shared what they learned (practice with a friend, check your slides twice, and take deep breaths), and asked others for their advice. The post got more traction than anything they'd done before, because everyone relates to flopping and trying again. That's what thought leadership really is: sharing the messy middle, not just the polished highlight reel.

Perfecting Your Angle

Finding your angle is more about being honest than being an expert. Think about the advice you wish someone had given you last year. Maybe it's how to deal with being ignored in meetings, or how to ask for feedback without sounding needy. Maybe it's a trick for keeping up with remote coworkers, or a story about a networking attempt that went totally sideways but turned out okay in the end. That stuff is gold. Jot down a few formats you could try: "how-to" guides (e.g., "How I Finally Got My Inbox Under Control"), "lessons learned" after a tough project, lists of your favorite apps or newsletters, or even quick takes on industry news from your point of view.

You don't need a fancy blog or hours of editing to share your thoughts. LinkedIn is your friend, and the posting tool is as easy as writing an email. Here's a simple formula: three paragraphs. Start with a hook ("Last week, I totally bombed my client call and learned three things."), explain what happened and what you learned, then end by asking others to share their tips or stories. If you're feeling brave, try Medium or leave thoughtful comments in industry forums. And don't stress if your first post doesn't go viral; showing up regularly matters a lot more.

If you want to stay organized (or just avoid that "what do I post?" panic), make a simple content calendar. It can be as basic as a spreadsheet with dates, topics, and a couple of checkboxes for "posted" and "followed up." This way, you can post regularly without burning out or repeating yourself. After you post, keep the conversation going. If someone comments ("I've been there, too!"), reply and ask how they handled it or if they have any advice you missed. If someone shares your post, send a quick thank you or connect for future ideas.

The secret isn't yelling into the void. It's talking to people. Like a few posts in your feed each week. Leave real comments, not just "Great post!" but something specific, like "Loved your point about setting boundaries in remote work. How did you handle it when your manager kept messaging after hours?" Share other people's resources, if they helped you, and tag them to give credit and start a conversation. Over time, these little things add up and show you're someone who cares, not someone who is just chasing likes.

Weekly Engagement Checklist

- Like/comment on three posts from peers in your field.
- Respond to every comment on your own posts.
- Share one helpful article or tool.
- Ask one follow-up question in a thread that interests you.

Thought leadership isn't just for gurus or influencers; it's for anyone willing to be helpful, honest, and a little bit brave online. Keep it real, keep it useful, and keep asking questions that get people talking instead of just clapping.

Managing Your Online Reputation and Digital Footprint

These days, your digital presence is your handshake, your reference check, and your first impression, all before you even know someone's looked you up. The good news is that you have more control over your online image than you think. Start with a quick "digital audit." Open an incognito browser and Google yourself (no logged-in accounts). Check a few pages of results using combos like your name plus your city, your job, or old usernames. Don't forget to check image search; sometimes those old photos pop up. Scroll through your public social media, including tagged photos and posts, so you know exactly what others see.

Once you know what's out there, it's cleanup time. Delete or archive old posts, such as arguments or jokes that don't sound like you anymore. If you find embarrassing photos, ask friends to untag you or tighten up your privacy settings. Update your bios so they match what you do now, not some old job or inside joke that doesn't help your professional image. Add a little personality: "Supply chain enthusiast/coffee snob helping teams deliver (literally)" beats "Just here for memes," but keep it in line with how you want to come across.

To stay ahead, get proactive. Set up Google Alerts for your name, common misspellings, or nicknames, so you'll know right away if something new pops up. If you spot something negative or weird, don't panic. Only respond if you really need to, and keep it professional: "Thanks for letting me know. I'm happy to explain what happened." If there's an awkward old post making the rounds, own it and move on: "Yep, that was me at the 2015 office karaoke contest. I've since retired my version of 'Don't Stop Believin'.'" Being honest about the past helps you steer your own story.

Make Sure You Are Consistent

Consistency is what makes your online presence believable. Make sure your LinkedIn, portfolio, Instagram bio (if it's public), and even smaller sites like GitHub or Notion all use a recent headshot: no baby photos or old conference selfies. Keep your message about what you do, what you care about, and who you are the same everywhere, both at work and outside it. If your LinkedIn says you're "passionate about building inclusive teams," make sure your other bios and posts back that up. Link your profiles so people can easily find you and get the full picture.

A consistent online presence makes you easier to remember and trust. If someone clicks from your LinkedIn to your portfolio to your X (formerly Twitter), they want to see the same person each time. If your profiles are all over the place, it just gets confusing and makes you look less credible. This doesn't mean you have to hide your real interests; just make sure everything fits together into one story.

Reputation Alignment Checklist

- Use the same headshot on LinkedIn, portfolio, and public social profiles.
- Match bios to your current job focus and values.
- Link between profiles for easy navigation.
- Ensure your first page of Google is free from off-brand or embarrassing content.
- Set up Google Alerts for ongoing monitoring.

Here's a real-life example: A friend noticed her X was all cat jokes, while her LinkedIn was super serious, "serious analyst" vibes. She added some humor to her LinkedIn ("Data sleuth by day, cat herder by night"), updated her headshots, and suddenly recruiters remembered her for all the right reasons.

Curating your online reputation isn't about hiding your personality or pretending you never had an awkward phase. It means you're helping people see who you are now and why they'd want to work with you. Clean up your digital footprint, keep your story straight across platforms, and check in now and then to keep things fresh. Once your online reputation lines up, you're ready to turn that credibility into real opportunities, the next step on your journey.

Chapter 8

Mastering Workplace Dynamics and Unwritten Rules

Decoding Company Culture: Reading the Signals That Matter

Starting a new job is a bit like showing up to a party where everyone's already deep in conversation, and you're the only one who didn't get the memo about the dress code. Maybe you spot the CEO rocking sneakers while you're sweating in your one "business casual" outfit, or you notice that in meetings, a handful of people do all the talking while the rest look like they're auditioning for a silent film. Pretty soon, it hits you: Doing your actual job is only half the battle. The other half? Figuring out the secret rules nobody bothered to write down. Forget the glossy handbook or the cheesy slogans on the office mugs. The real culture is hiding in Slack threads, whispered side chats, and the mysterious way certain people always get a shoutout when things go right.

Every workplace has its own secret code, and it's usually not printed anywhere you can find it. If you don't crack it fast, you'll end up doing something awkward, like hitting reply-all to the whole company or showing up in a blazer when everyone else is in hoodies.

Here's the move: Don't just listen to what the higher-ups say; watch what they *do*. If your boss is all about "work-life balance" but pings you at midnight, you've got your answer. Notice who gets the fist bumps, the team players or the lone wolves? Who gets invited to the after-meeting meeting? Who's always left out when it's time to celebrate? These little patterns are the real rulebook.

Pay Attention During Meetings

If you want to crack the code, channel your inner detective. Meetings are basically a goldmine for clues: Who jumps in with ideas, and who looks like they're counting ceiling tiles? Do the same three people always steer the conversation, or does everyone get a shot? Even the way people roll their eyes or trade glances can tell you who's really running the show. Online, it's all about the vibe. Are people tossing around high-five emojis, or is it all dry thumbs-ups and "per my last email"? How fast do people reply? Is the tone friendly, or does it feel like everyone's writing to the IRS? All these little habits are your cheat sheet for what flies and what's a no-go.

Unwritten rules are the kind that sneak up and smack you in the face if you're not paying attention. Like, is it cool to send a Slack at 10 p.m., or will that get you side-eyed into next week? The only way to know is to try it: Send a message after hours and see if your phone lights up like a Christmas tree or if it's crickets until morning. Meetings are another clue: Are they free-for-alls where everyone's tossing out ideas, or does it feel like you're watching a one-person show? And don't even get me started on remote dress codes. Are people in hoodies and bedhead, or is someone still rocking a tie on Zoom? What people wear tells you how much anyone cares about appearances.

Even the way people talk (or type) is its own secret language. Is your team all about quick DMs, or do they write emails longer than your college essays? Are GIFs and jokes flying around, or is it all business, all the time? When there's a disagreement, do people hash it out or pretend nothing happened? Save yourself some awkward moments and ask early: "How do people usually give feedback here?" or "What's the best way to pitch a new idea?" It shows you're paying attention and saves you from stepping in it later.

Advancement often follows a hidden script as well. Promotions and recognition might not depend on annual reviews or tenure but on informal processes like project involvement or networking. Ask a colleague, "How do promotions usually work here?" The answer can help you plan your next career step with clearer expectations.

Culture Decoder Checklist

- Watch what leaders do, not just what they say.
- Note who gets recognized and why.
- Observe who participates in meetings.
- Monitor emoji use, response speed, and message tone online.
- Test after-hours communication expectations.
- Check dress cues on calls and in person.
- Clarify feedback and idea-sharing practices.
- Ask questions to fill in your knowledge gaps.
- Find out how promotions and advancement really happen.

Workplace culture is the secret sauce that decides who gets noticed, who gets the cool projects, and how hard you have to work just to feel like you belong. The faster you pick up on the signals, the less time you'll spend second-guessing yourself, and the more you'll feel like you actually know what you're doing.

How Work Really Gets Done
(Beyond the Job Description)

Unwritten Rules *(Culture Signals)*	Influence & Politics *(Power Flow)*	Visibility & Advocacy *(Especially Remote)*
• Meetings: who speaks, who decides • Communication: tone, speed, emojis vs formality • Norms: hours, dress, *feedback* style	• Formal leaders vs informal influencers • Gatekeepers & allies • Where decisions actually happen	• Making work visible • Updates, documentation, brag files • Sponsorship & recognition

———————— Advancement ————————

Understanding Office Politics (Without Losing Your Integrity)

Most people don't start a new job eager to play office politics, but like it or not, every workplace has an unofficial system of influence and alliance. Office politics isn't about drama; it's about knowing how work gets done, who makes the real decisions, and how resources flow. Think of it as the hidden menu at your favorite restaurant. Ignore it, and you risk being sidelined from projects, important conversations, and even promotions. The real trick is to play smart, not dirty.

Start by figuring out who really holds influence in your office. Don't concentrate solely on job titles; it's often the assistant who knows everyone's schedule or the project manager who always gets their way. Watch who gets listened to in meetings, whose opinion is sought before decisions, and who seems to know what's next. These informal power players, gatekeepers, influencers, and quiet allies are worth mapping out. For visual thinkers, a simple chart can help. Remember, allies can be anyone: an IT technician who can expedite requests, or someone in HR with advance notice on team changes. Knowing who's really in the loop makes your efforts more effective.

You don't have to become a manipulator to thrive. Building political capital can be positive. Volunteering for cross-team projects gains exposure and builds a reputation as a helpful collaborator, not someone stuck in their silo. Active listening in meetings matters. People notice who genuinely hears them out; it creates goodwill and helps position you as a valuable team member when the going gets tough.

Even if schmoozing isn't your style, you can authentically build influence. Find the team "glue" people and seek their advice when needed. Rather than trying to impress every manager, connect authentically by helping others with tight deadlines, sharing useful resources, or paying close attention in meetings and recapping action points. Small, authentic efforts accumulate, making you a go-to colleague.

Watch Out for the Dark Side

The darker side of office politics includes gossip, cliques, and favoritism. To keep a clean reputation, avoid negativity without coming off as aloof. When talk turns gossipy, try: "I'd rather focus on finishing this project," or "I don't know the full story, so I'll stay out of it." This approach sets boundaries and keeps your reputation trustworthy. If you encounter favoritism, maybe a coworker who always gets the best assignments, don't immediately confront them. Instead, focus on doing excellent work, document your contributions, and proactively seek out stretch opportunities from other teams or leaders. Staying visible and expanding your network can help shift workplace dynamics in your favor.

Protecting your reputation also means resisting the temptation to vent about colleagues or managers, especially in private DMs or chats, as digital records are permanent. If someone tries to involve you in drama or negative talk, stay neutral: "I haven't noticed," or "I'm just trying to focus on my work." People remember those who stay above petty conflicts and are more likely to entrust major responsibilities to them later.

I've seen firsthand how damaging gossip can be, even when people think they're being "private." As a manager, I once dealt with a situation where two employees were emailing negatively about a coworker, assuming it would never leave their inboxes. It did. The coworker found out, came to me in tears, and told me she was ready to quit. What followed was uncomfortable for everyone involved. I immediately brought in their direct manager, and the employees responsible were confronted with the real impact of their actions. They weren't defensive; they were devastated. What they thought was harmless venting turned into a moment that damaged trust, morale, and working relationships. It was a clear reminder that gossip doesn't just "stay between us," and the consequences are rarely abstract. That once damaged, reputations are hard to repair.

Advocating for yourself doesn't require stepping on others or fighting for credit at every turn. When there's conflict over resources or recognition, suggest win-win solutions: "Maybe we can split the budget and share outcomes?" or "Let's present our parts together so everyone can contribute." When arguments heat up, sometimes it's best to step back rather than escalate, especially if your involvement won't change the outcome or could harm relationships.

Strong ethics are especially important during workplace tension. When disagreements arise, or rumors start, stay focused on collective goals: "Let's aim to deliver this on time," or "Everyone's input matters before we decide." Avoid drama triangles, situations where people talk about others instead of talking directly to them. If you sense conflict brewing but don't have the facts, silence is often best; other times, consult your manager for advice on a constructive way forward.

Ultimately, successfully managing office politics means blending awareness with authenticity and being strategic about relationships, but never manipulative. Build influence by being reliable, helpful, and fair. Safeguard your reputation by steering clear of gossip. Advocate for yourself by creating solutions that benefit both you and your team. The goal isn't to outmaneuver colleagues, but to advance together while keeping your integrity and your sanity intact.

Remote-First Workplaces: Visibility, Advocacy, and Advancement

Working in a remote-first company can feel a bit like shouting into the void while wearing noise-canceling headphones. The "out of sight, out of mind" problem isn't just a cliché; it's a legit challenge. When you're not bumping into your boss in the break room or getting that casual "great work" after a big meeting, it's way too easy to become invisible. The lack of spontaneous recognition can leave you feeling like your best work is just floating around in cyberspace, unappreciated and unnoticed. Your projects might launch smoothly, but you're left wondering if anyone even saw the fireworks.

To stay visible, you need to be proactive, not pushy. Regular status updates and progress summaries aren't just for show; they're your digital "Hey, look what I did!" Instead of waiting for someone to ask, send a quick summary at the end of each week. Keep it punchy: what you accomplished, what you're working on, and where you need input. Share wins as soon as they happen, even if it's just a Slack message: "Wrapped up the client dashboard ahead of schedule. Let me know if you'd like a walkthrough!" For important meetings, don't be that mysterious black square. Turn your camera on, even if your hair's a mess, and make eye contact with the screen. Nod, react, use emojis, anything to remind folks you're a living person, not just another calendar invite.

Building credibility remotely means showing up consistently and making your results visible. If you're leading a project, record a quick Loom video to demo progress or highlight challenges. Post updates in team channels so others can chime in or cheer you on. Don't wait for managers to notice your work; make it easy for them by giving them the "TL;DR" (too long, didn't read) version up front. Be the person who makes information accessible and keeps stakeholders in the loop. Over time, this habit builds trust and positions you as reliable, which helps counter any doubts about what you're really doing from your home office.

Preparation and Readiness

Visibility works best when it's backed by preparation. Managers quickly notice who truly knows their work inside and out. When you anticipate follow-up questions, understand your numbers, and can clearly explain not just what you did but why it mattered, trust builds fast. Even when the questions never come, that level of readiness shows, and it often leads to more responsibility and autonomy.

Advocating for yourself remotely takes intentional effort, but it doesn't have to feel awkward or self-promotional. Ask directly for stretch projects: "I saw we're starting that new initiative. Could I help with the rollout?" If you want more responsibility but aren't sure how to bring it up, send your manager an email outlining your recent impact and ask what higher-level work you can take on in the next quarter. Use digital dashboards (Google Sheets, Notion) or "brag docs," living documents where you log completed projects, feedback from colleagues, and measurable results. Share these during one-on-ones or quarterly reviews so your achievements don't get lost in the shuffle.

Sponsorships work a little differently at a distance, but they're still possible. Reach out to leaders outside your direct team when you finish something impressive by sending a short note with context

("We launched a new feature; here's the early feedback and why it matters"). This puts your name in their mind when new opportunities arise and signals that you're thinking beyond your daily tasks. If your company has recognition channels or shoutout threads, nominate teammates and occasionally share group wins, which shows leadership and helps build goodwill.

When it comes to advancement, you can't rely on hallway chats or being "seen" working late. Schedule regular career check-ins with your manager. Don't assume they know your ambitions just because you're doing solid work. Put time on their calendar every few months to discuss growth: What skills should you build next? What gaps do they see before promotion? Ask for feedback on recent projects and how to step into more visible roles. Frame these conversations around your impact: "I've streamlined our reporting process. What else can I own that would move the needle for our team?" This keeps your name top of mind when new roles open or when leadership discusses succession planning.

Remote promotion-readiness requires signaling value over time; it is not a one-off conversation. Build a track record of delivering results, communicating clearly, and stepping up when others hesitate. Keep documentation of your contributions up to date so you're ready when opportunities pop up unexpectedly.

Remote Promotion-Readiness Checklist

- Are you sharing regular updates with both your manager and wider team?
- Can you point to a quantifiable impact from recent projects?
- Have you asked for (and received) feedback on growth areas?
- Do leaders outside your direct team know who you are?

- Are your skills visible and documented beyond Slack or Zoom?
- Have you articulated your interest in promotion or new responsibilities?

Remote work doesn't have to mean flying under the radar. With intentional habits like clear updates, strategic advocacy, and scheduled growth conversations, you'll stay visible and build momentum no matter where your desk is.

Advocating for Yourself: Scripts and Tactics for Recognition

Have you ever felt like your hard work at the office goes unnoticed? You might finish a big project or land a new client, only for the credit to bypass you. The truth is, recognition rarely comes by accident. Advocate for it without becoming that person who boasts about every detail. The key is learning to speak up naturally, collaboratively, and authentically.

Prepare a few scripts that fit your style and highlight your efforts without sounding boastful. After a project win, try: "I wanted to share a quick win from last week's project. I streamlined our process, and we cut production time by 20%. Happy to show the team how I approached it if that's helpful." In meetings where your role might be overlooked, say, "Could we include my contribution to the kickoff phase in the project recap? I think it helps show the full team effort." These brief comments can reshape how your impact is remembered.

Don't just hope people remember your contributions; keep a "brag file." This is a simple running list of achievements, big and small, that you update regularly. It can be a document, a Notion page, or a folder in your email where you jot down wins, positive feedback, or tricky problems you solved, with dates and short descriptions. When it's time for a performance review, a raise request, or a conversation about more responsibility, you'll have your case built already, and you won't be scrambling through emails trying to compile what you've done. I have found that keeping an updated list of my accomplishments makes a real difference around review time. It helps me stand out without overselling myself and shows my manager that I take pride in my work. More importantly, I'm no longer scrambling or relying on memory or old reviews to make my case.

Take it a step further by occasionally sending your manager a short self-review, even when you haven't been asked. Keep it brief and focused, highlighting three main wins, what you learned, and one area you want to grow next. For example: "This quarter, I led the launch campaign for Product Z (resulting in a 15% sales bump), onboarded two new team members, and streamlined our reporting process. I'm proud of these results and would like to build more leadership responsibility next."

Most people do not realize that almost no one does this outside of formal review season. In years of corporate life, I rarely saw employees proactively summarize their impact without being prompted, which is exactly why it stands out. When done well, it does not come across as ego-driven. It reads as organized, self-aware, and leadership-ready. You are not asking your manager to hunt for your impact. You are making it easy to see.

Self-Advocacy and Advocacy From Others

Peer recognition and 360-degree feedback are valuable, too. If self-promotion feels awkward, encouragement from colleagues can make a big difference. After working together, you might ask, "If my input was helpful, would you mind letting [manager] know? It would mean a lot." Participate in shoutout channels or meetings if your company uses them; giving kudos to others also encourages reciprocity. Public recognition of others boosts morale and helps create a culture where everyone's contributions are acknowledged.

If you're introverted or from a background where self-advocacy feels uncomfortable or risky, try reframing it as team advocacy: "Highlighting this process improvement could help us all save time next quarter." If direct praise is hard, enlist a mentor or sponsor: "I feel awkward bringing this up, but would you be open to mentioning my role in the project during our next team meeting?" This way, a more senior voice can endorse your work while you build your comfort level.

An employee who once dreaded attention started emailing monthly results and outcomes to her boss after a peer suggested it. No embellishment, just facts and numbers. Months later, those summaries played a key role in her performance review and helped her finally secure a raise.

Advocating for yourself isn't about boasting; it's about ensuring your efforts aren't overlooked. When in doubt, stick to facts and tie your results to team progress: "I wanted to share [result] because it might help us all [benefit]." Or ask someone you trust to speak up for you. Your work deserves recognition; don't let it fade into the background.

Leveraging Diversity: Turning Unique Backgrounds Into Career Assets

If you've ever felt like the odd one out at work, maybe because you grew up in a different country, speak another language at home, or took a winding path to your field, you might have wondered if your background is something to downplay during meetings. It's tempting to try to blend in, especially early in your career, but the truth is, teams need people who bring new perspectives. Companies aren't just paying lip service here. There's real evidence that teams with a mix of backgrounds generate better ideas, spot risks sooner, and connect with broader markets. Major organizations look for this edge. Ever notice tech firms talking about "diversity of thought" when launching a feature? Or global brands assembling multicultural teams to adapt products for different markets? It's not charity; it's strategy.

Your own experiences, whether cultural, linguistic, or even life struggles, shape how you look at problems and find solutions. Maybe you grew up translating for family, which makes you a natural at reading between the lines and picking up subtle cues others miss. Perhaps you've switched careers or moved countries and learned to quickly adapt, making you more flexible when projects go sideways. The real opportunity is learning to spot these skills and frame them in ways that show value to your team or boss. A quick framework: Jot down unique experiences you've had (moving cities, first in your family to finish college, organizing community events), then link each one to a workplace skill or advantage. For example: "My experience navigating two cultures helps me spot misunderstandings before they become problems," or "Being bilingual lets me help our team connect with global clients."

Start With This Quick Worksheet

1. What's something about my background or upbringing that shaped how I see the world?
2. How has that helped me solve problems or connect with others at work?
3. What have I done that most people on my team haven't?
4. How could this experience help our team succeed or innovate?

Now, let's talk about communicating these strengths without sounding like you're reading from a TED Talk script. When sharing your story in interviews or meetings, keep it simple and relevant. If someone asks about your approach to challenges, say: "My background in [A] has taught me to approach [B] differently. For example, when we ran into issues with our overseas partner, I drew on my experience working across cultures to smooth things over." You're not bragging; you're showing why your experiences make you an asset.

Take the case of Miguel, a first-generation college grad who joined a global company. He grew up speaking Spanish at home and English everywhere else. Instead of hiding his accent or background, he volunteered to help translate documents and bridge gaps between teams in different countries. Soon, his manager put him on international projects, and when the company expanded into Latin America, Miguel was the go-to person for strategy sessions. What looked like a "difference" turned into a shortcut to promotion.

You might still run into bias or stereotypes, including subtle or not-so-subtle microaggressions. The trick is to respond in ways that flip the script. If someone makes a comment like, "Oh, you probably don't get our inside jokes," try: "Actually, my experience in [A] helps our team understand [B] market, and that's come in handy more than once." Turn awkward moments into teaching opportunities or clear reminders of what you bring.

Building support networks is also important. Find other underrepresented colleagues, even if it's just a Slack channel or coffee group, and trade notes on your various challenges. You're stronger together. You can find allies just about anywhere: people who listen, share credit, or speak up when others cross the line. Keep a mental checklist: Who supports your growth? Who listens when you speak? Who stands up for inclusion? These allies help amplify your voice and can even open doors you didn't know existed.

Sometimes what feels like your biggest difference is actually your secret weapon. The project manager who grew up as the only woman in her engineering class now leads workshops on inclusive design. The coder who speaks three languages helps the team break into new markets without needing outside translators. These aren't exceptions; they're everyday examples of turning so-called weaknesses into leadership opportunities.

Remember that every career has twists and turns, but those twists often become your best stories and strongest selling points. Don't shrink from what makes you different; let it take center stage when it matters. As we move forward into the next chapter, think about how you can use your unique perspective not just to fit in, but to stand out and drive real momentum in your career.

Chapter 9

Sustainable Success, Boundaries, and Burnout-Proofing

Early Warning Signs of Burnout (And What to Do Next)

It's Monday morning, your alarm is screaming, and you're already tired before your feet hit the floor. Remember when you had energy for work? Yeah, me too. Now it's more like running on fumes and hoping for the best. If that sounds familiar, you might be inching toward burnout. It doesn't usually show up with fireworks; it sneaks in, disguised as regular old stress, until one day you realize you're completely wiped out.

Burnout isn't just some buzzword HR throws around; it's a real thing, especially if you care about your job and also want to keep your sanity. Spotting the early signs is like noticing your car's check engine light before you end up stranded on the side of the road. The first clues usually show up in your body: You're always tired, maybe your head hurts, your stomach's off, or you wake up feeling like you barely slept. You might snap at people over nothing, lose patience with clients, or feel your usual spark fizzling out. If you catch yourself dreading work or not even caring about the free snacks anymore, that's a red flag. And if you're procrastinating, zoning out in meetings, or using food and Netflix as your escape plan, you're not alone. Feeling like you're just going through the motions? Yep, that's another big clue.

We briefly introduced these early warning signs back in Chapter 1 when talking about sustainable success. Here, we're slowing down and looking at them more closely so you can recognize burnout before it starts calling the shots.

Burnout Early Warning Checklist: How Many Can You Tick?

- Waking up tired every day despite sleeping
- Dreading work by Sunday evening
- Getting irritable at coworkers/clients
- Losing interest in projects you once enjoyed
- Struggling to focus or complete tasks
- Physical complaints (headaches, stomach issues)
- Procrastinating or doom-scrolling
- Feeling like your achievements no longer matter

Stages of Burnout

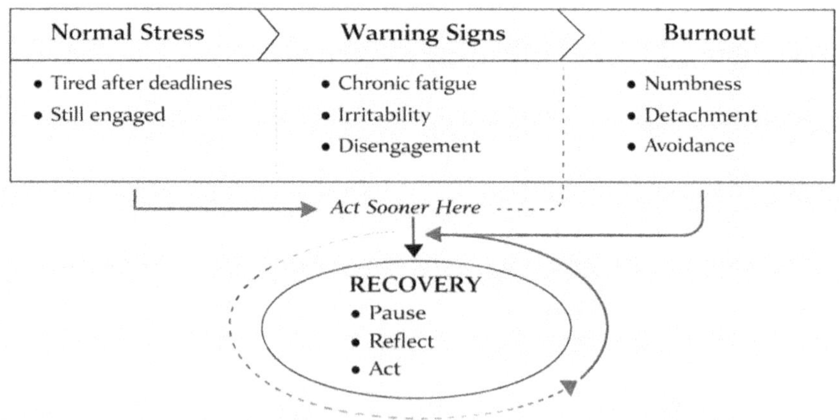

How do you tell regular stress from chronic burnout? Stress is often linked to specific events or deadlines ("big presentation next week") and comes and goes. Burnout is a lingering state; it sticks around long after major events, making even simple tasks overwhelming. Stress leaves you anxious but engaged; burnout leaves you feeling empty and detached. You care about doing well, but simply can't summon the energy or focus.

Take Melissa, a new grad excited for her tech job. At first, she dove into everything: extra projects, late-night emails, and being a team player. After six months, she started hitting snooze, stopped volunteering, and became snappy with friends. She realized her spark was going out, and that it was not just tiredness, but actual burnout.

If any of this sounds like you, don't just brush it off. Here's a quick game plan: Pause, reflect, and act. First, stop and admit what's going on (I know, easier said than done). Then, grab a notebook or your phone and ask yourself: *What's draining my energy? When was the last time I felt excited about work? Is this a new thing, or has it been building up?* Finally, do one small thing today: Take a real lunch break, schedule a mental health day if you can, or try out a mood-tracking app. If your job has an Employee Assistance Program, jot down their number now, not just when things hit the fan.

If you need to speak up at work, remember: Asking for help is smart, not weak. If you need to bring workload issues to HR or your manager, keep it direct: "I've noticed I'm not feeling like myself and wanted to discuss possible adjustments." Or write: "Hi [Manager], I'd like to request a mental health day to recharge and ensure I'm at my best. Please let me know if any paperwork is required." If talking in person is daunting, try writing first. The key is opening the conversation. Most managers would rather help than see you burn out. If the phrase "mental health day" feels uncomfortable, using "personal day" works just as well.

- **Pause:** Where do you feel stress in your body right now?
- **Journal prompt:** What's one thing that would make work easier this week?
- **Resource list:** National EAP hotline; Headspace or Calm app for mindfulness breaks; Mayo Clinic burnout guide

Burnout is a sneaky little gremlin, but if you catch it early and do something about it, you can get back on track.

Setting Boundaries Up, Down, and Across Teams

Think of boundaries as the invisible fences that keep your work brain from gobbling up your whole life (and your sanity). They're the key to long-term survival and thriving at work. Want to still care about your job five years from now? Boundaries aren't a nice-to-have; they're a must. People who set clear limits at work tend to be less stressed and more productive. Their energy doesn't disappear by Wednesday, and their teams tend to respect them more. Turns out, drawing the line means you take both your job and your well-being seriously.

Setting boundaries can get tricky because no two work relationships are exactly the same. Your manager isn't your peer, and your peers aren't your direct reports. Each requires its own approach. Think of it as choosing the right tool for the job. With a manager, boundaries often mean clarifying expectations around response times, task priorities, and after-hours requests. For example, if your boss has a habit of sending Slack messages at midnight (and expects an answer before sunrise), you can address this with a calm, direct conversation: "I've noticed late-night messages are becoming more frequent.

I want to make sure I'm delivering my best work during normal hours. Can we agree on urgent versus non-urgent communication?" When working with peers, boundaries are about protecting focus time and avoiding the infamous "just a quick question" rabbit hole. A simple boundary might sound like: "I'm heads-down on a tight deadline this afternoon, but I can help after 2 p.m." With direct reports, you need to set clear guidelines for availability, letting them know when you're open for questions and when you need uninterrupted time to tackle your own tasks.

To make these boundaries stick without sounding defensive or like you're building a brick wall around yourself, communicate with them clearly and kindly. Email templates are your friend here. If you want to set office hours or clarify when you'll respond to requests, try something like: "Hi team! I'll be doing focused work from 9 to 11 a.m. each day, so responses may be delayed until after. For urgent needs, please mark as high priority or ping me on Slack after 11." For after-hours texts or emails, set expectations up front: "I check messages until 6 p.m.; anything after that will be picked up first thing in the morning." On Slack or Teams, status updates can do a lot of heavy lifting: "In focus mode, back online after lunch!" or "Working on deadline, ping if urgent." These small signals train others about how and when to reach you, gently nudging them to respect your calendar.

You don't need to use all of these. Even one clear boundary makes a difference.

When Boundaries Are Tested

Of course, boundaries will sometimes get tested by managers who "forget," colleagues who thrive on interruptions, or reports who treat every question as an emergency. When that happens, troubleshooting is key. If someone repeatedly crosses a line you've set, even after reminders, start documenting what's happening.

Keep a quick log: date, time, what was requested, and how you responded. It's important to have all your facts straight if you need to escalate later. If you need to revisit an earlier conversation, keep it simple and non-confrontational: "I wanted to circle back on our discussion about response times. I've noticed a few urgent requests after hours lately. Can we talk about how to handle future priorities?" If things still don't improve, and it's impacting your work or well-being, loop in HR or a trusted support contact. You might say: "I've tried setting limits with [Person], but haven't seen change. Can we discuss options for support?" This isn't tattling; it's advocating for yourself and modeling healthy boundaries for everyone else feeling the same pain.

Creating a boundary-setting matrix can help you think through what works for each relationship. With managers, clarify response windows and priority signals. With peers, set focus blocks and communicate clearly about availability. With direct reports, provide office hours and model healthy habits. Templates can be tweaked for every scenario and adapted as needed until they feel natural. The reality is that most people want guidance; they just need you to set the tone.

Setting boundaries takes time, like learning how to ride a bike and dealing with wobbles and awkward moments. That's totally normal. The trick is to stick with it and remember you're not just looking out for yourself. You're showing everyone else it's okay to set limits, too, which makes the whole team work better and keeps the drama to a minimum. Best of all, boundaries give you space to breathe and enjoy your job, and your life outside of it.

Saying No Without Career Risk: Scripts for Workload and Priorities

If you've ever found yourself agreeing to projects when your to-do list is already overflowing, you know the struggle. The pressure to say yes to everything can seem like a badge of ambition and commitment, but in truth, saying no is one of the most underrated career skills. Don't think of it as laziness; you're protecting your focus to deliver your best work, not just more work. Consider the project manager who set boundaries: "I'm at capacity right now, but let's revisit this after this sprint." Their projects landed on time, the team avoided chaos, and their boss trusted them more.

Refusing extra work isn't always easy, especially when asked by someone senior or when you fear seeming unhelpful. But your career shouldn't run on guilt or fear of missing out. You can set boundaries and still be seen as reliable, dedicated, and promotable. Here are some simple scripts to help avoid awkwardness or endless apologizing:

- "Thanks for thinking of me! I'm at capacity with A and B right now, but if this can wait until next week, I'd love to help."
- "Can we revisit this after the current project wraps up? My plate is full, and I want to give this the attention it deserves."
- "I want to do this well, but I can't take it on without letting something else slip. What's the priority?"

These can be adjusted whether you're talking to your boss, a peer, or a report.

You might not need a hard "no"; sometimes, just negotiating helps. If a last-minute deadline lands on your desk, try: "If this is urgent, which current task should I deprioritize?" This makes your workload visible to others and forces a choice. If collaboration is an option, try:

"Could we split the work or loop someone else in?" Or: "I'd like to support this, but my plate is full. Can we set a more realistic timeline?" One junior employee improved their project quality this way, negotiating staggered delivery dates instead of agreeing to every request. Not only did they avoid burnout, but their manager also noticed the improvement and started assigning them more strategic work instead of nonstop busywork.

Fearing Your Reputation

The biggest fear with saying no usually isn't about workload; it's reputational. You might worry that turning something down means getting labeled as difficult or being passed over for promotions. In practice, people who set limits and communicate priorities tend to be seen as reliable and focused, qualities managers value when it comes to advancement. Managers value someone who delivers what's promised over a stretched-thin yes-person. Employees who communicate boundaries not only protect their sanity; they often get promoted. Teams respect honesty, clients appreciate realistic timelines, and leadership sees you as trustworthy.

If pushback scares you, remember that saying no doesn't mean you are rejecting something or someone. Rather, you are protecting your ability to do great work and stay sane. If someone challenges your refusal, restate your capacity: "I want to help when I can. Right now, I'm focused on A and B. Let's look at this in a couple of days." If guilt is used ("But we need all hands!"), calmly reiterate priorities: "I understand it's urgent. To do my best work, I'd need to shift something else off my list." This isn't selfish; this is smart, responsible professionalism.

Every time you say yes to something, you're saying no to something else: maybe it's sleep, maybe it's doing your job well, or maybe it's just your sanity. Your time and energy aren't unlimited, no matter how much coffee you drink. If you want to keep showing up for what matters (and not become the go-to fixer for everything), treat your time like it's gold. It's not just about mental health; you're playing the long game at work.

Plug-and-Play Scripts and Resilience Quick Guide

- **For managers:** "To take this on now, I'd need to delay [current project]. Which should take priority?"
- **For peers:** "I'd love to help! Can we tag-team or stagger deadlines?"
- **For direct reports:** "Let's find another way so neither of us gets overloaded."
- **Resilience tip:** Every time you set a limit and stick to it, you build credibility not just with others, but with yourself.

Saying no isn't a risk; it's how you build a sustainable career and a reputation for the right reasons.

Work-Life Integration: Customizing Balance for Your Reality

Yes, "work-life balance" sounds amazing, but real life is much messier than some perfect 50/50 split. That old idea of clocking out at 5 p.m. and instantly becoming your off-duty self? For most of us, that's pure fantasy. Instead, think of work and life as a sliding scale. Some days, work takes over; other days, you can focus on your own stuff. The trick is to build your own version of balance, a setup that fits your real life, not some Instagram highlight reel. Imagine a spectrum: On one end, you're all work and deadlines; on the other, you're deep in personal time, maybe hiking or just binge-watching Netflix. Most days, you'll land somewhere in the middle, and that's totally fine.

Start by figuring out your energy patterns and what you absolutely refuse to give up, your non-negotiables. These are the things that keep you sane, even when work is extra loud. Maybe it's family dinners, your weekly soccer game, or a chunk of time for painting or gaming. Grab a notebook or your phone and do a quick energy check: When do you feel most awake? (Some people peak at sunrise, others are basically nocturnal.) Notice your weekly patterns, too. Maybe Wednesday afternoons are always zombie mode, and you need a recharge. Make a simple chart with these labels: "High Energy," "Low Energy," and "Non-Negotiables." Mark which times are best for deep work and which are for fun. By filling this out, you are learning how to work with your natural rhythms, not against them.

Once you know your best times for work and play, guard them like a bouncer at a VIP club. Block out time on your calendar, not just for meetings but for your own priorities too. Make space for exercise, lunch with friends, or just zoning out to music. Be sure to put these things on your schedule, because if they're not there, they probably won't happen. If you work from home or freelance, maybe that means a midday walk or a set creative hour. If you're a parent, maybe it's bedtime routines or school pickups. The goal isn't to be perfect; it's to have some predictability, so you know you'll get what you need most.

Tech boundaries matter, too. If you're answering emails at midnight or scrolling through Slack when you should be sleeping, it's time for a device curfew. Try app blockers to keep after-hours work stuff from sneaking in. Some people swear by "Do Not Disturb" after 7 p.m.; others toss their phone in another room after work. Experiment until you find what works for you. It might feel awkward at first (like, will your boss notice if you don't reply in five seconds?), but people usually get used to your new habits, and most of the time, they respect them.

For me, this boundary was simple and non-negotiable. I never took work home with me. I didn't reply to work texts after I left the office, and I never brought my laptop home. That didn't mean I watched the clock or left at the same time every day. If something needed to get done, I stayed later and finished it. But once I left, work stayed at work. Home was home.

That rule protected my personal life and, surprisingly, made me more reliable at work. People knew that when I was there, I was fully present and focused. And because I handled things thoroughly before leaving, there was rarely a reason for anything to spill into my evenings. That separation kept burnout at bay and helped me show up consistently, day after day, without feeling like work was slowly taking over everything else.

Making It Work for You

I've seen professionals totally reimagine their routines by getting creative with integration. One remote worker I know realized she hit a wall every afternoon around 2 p.m., so she started taking brisk walks instead of forcing herself through another meeting. Her energy picked up, her focus improved, and by the end of the day, she was less grumpy at home. Another friend juggled freelance gigs alongside a full-time job by carving out strict "side-hustle sprints," short bursts after dinner only on Mondays and Thursdays, which let him keep his weekends sacred for recharging and social life.

Sometimes, companies talk a big game about balance but don't actually protect it (cue the endless "work hard, play hard" posters in break rooms no one uses). In those environments, sustainable success means creating your own systems behind the scenes. Take the case of someone I know who worked in fast-paced finance, where after-hours emails were the norm and "balance" was code for "don't complain." She secretly built personal rules: never missing weekly family dinners, using her lunch break for reading (not work), and never booking meetings after 4 p.m. if she could help it. She managed her energy by organizing projects around these non-negotiables and declined to apologize if she didn't answer pings after hours. She simply replied in the morning with consistent quality work. Her performance reviews stayed strong year after year because her system kept her sharp and reliable, even when the office culture didn't.

The truth is, real work-life balance rarely comes from some official policy. It's built on a bunch of small choices, routines you protect, and being honest with yourself about what matters most. Your version of balance will look different from everyone else's, and that's not just okay; it's the whole point. What matters is finding that sweet spot where your job supports your life, not steamrolls it.

Resilience Routines: Mental Health, Reflection, and Recovery Strategies

Resilience is more than just a buzzword; it's how you bounce back when work gets tough. The core of resilience is your brain's neuroplasticity, its ability to adapt and form new pathways. By practicing resilience skills, you're not just enduring stress, but training your mind to recover faster and grow stronger. Think of your brain as a muscle; each time you use a new coping tool or build a positive habit, you're making it more resilient. This means setbacks don't define you, and failures aren't final.

Building resilience starts with simple, consistent habits. Reflection is a key tool: Spend five minutes at the end of each day jotting down what went well, what didn't, and what you learned. Make it casual, not a formal task. Use gratitude prompts such as "What was one good thing that happened today?" or "Who helped me out this week?" Focusing on positive moments conditions your brain to notice the good, even on stressful days. Another useful strategy is conducting regular progress check-ins. What did you accomplish this week that would have made you proud months ago? Over time, this shows your growth and not just your setbacks.

Mindfulness can be simple and part of your daily routine. For most professionals, micro-practices work best: Take three deep breaths between meetings, close your eyes for a minute at lunch and listen to your surroundings, or slow down and really taste your morning coffee. These brief pauses help your brain recover from constant stimuli and demands. Schedule occasional "digital detoxes"; turn off notifications and put your phone away for an hour. When your mind has room to wander, you might discover creative solutions or simply feel more refreshed.

Everyone faces setbacks and disappointments at work. Resilient people don't avoid these, but bounce back by focusing on learning. After a failure, try a quick reflection: *What happened? Which parts were under my control? What can I try differently next time?* Stay focused on solutions, not self-blame. If you're stuck, reach out to a mentor or peer for perspective; most people are happy to help and appreciate your openness about learning.

Support groups matter, too. Whether it's a professional Slack channel, local meetup, or just a group chat with friends who understand your work struggles, sharing experiences helps. Explore mental health resources made for young professionals: online counseling, peer support hotlines, or well-being apps that check on your mood and guide short meditations. Make a go-to list of such resources so you know where to turn in rough patches.

Making a Plan

It helps to formalize a "personal resilience plan": Identify common work stressors (deadlines, feedback, communication overload), then list coping strategies that genuinely help you cope (opt for a walk, chat with a friend, or do something creative). Make note of two or three people you'd reach out to when things get tough, whether it's a mentor, trusted coworker, or supportive friend.

For example, after being laid off from a job he loved, one analyst started each morning journaling about what he could control; he made weekly calls with a former coworker for mutual support, and in the evenings, he chose outdoor activities or creative hobbies over endless job searches. The routine didn't cure everything, but kept his mindset adaptable and hopeful until he found a new role.

Resilience is like Wi-Fi for your career: easy to overlook when it's strong but essential when times get tough. Develop these habits now so you're ready for challenges, both at work and beyond. Next, we'll move from day-to-day survival to building leverage for long-term career advancement, while protecting your well-being.

Chapter 10

Action Plans, Momentum, and Career Growth Check-Ins

The Career Growth Action Plan: Quarterly Goals and Reviews

Checking your career plan just once a year is basically the work version of letting your fridge go for months, and suddenly you're staring at a science experiment that used to be spinach. Real progress doesn't come from grand, New Year's–style promises or vague "someday" plans. It's all about those small, regular check-ins, like catching your veggies before they turn into compost. That's why quarterly career action planning works: It gives your big dreams some structure, breaks them into steps you can tackle, and lets you fix things before they go totally off the rails.

We've all set those wild goals, "I'll be a negotiation wizard!" or "Promotion, here I come!" and then watched our motivation fizzle out by February. Quarterly planning is like taking those big, intimidating dreams and shrinking them down to something you can actually do. The trick? SMART goals. Yes, it sounds like corporate speak, but trust me, having goals that are specific, measurable, achievable, rele-

147

vant, and time-bound is what keeps your plans from turning into wishful thinking.

So, instead of the classic, fuzzy goal of "get more recognition," a SMART goal sounds more like, "By the end of Q2, I'll present my project results at two team meetings and send monthly updates to leadership." Suddenly, you've got something you can actually do, not just hope for. The same goes for learning new skills ("Finish an online SQL course and use it on a real project by June 30th") or making a career pivot ("Do three informational interviews in product management and update my LinkedIn before the quarter's over").

Kick off each quarter by picking one to three things to focus on, maybe a skill you want to build, a project you want to tackle, or a step toward a bigger change. Write out your SMART goals and put them somewhere you'll see them (your phone wallpaper or a sticky note on your laptop counts). Then break each goal into monthly chunks: What do you need to get done this month? What about next month? If you're working on a skill, maybe that means blocking out time each week for a course or practicing something new. If you're aiming for a promotion, maybe it's time to chat with your manager about your growth plan, volunteer for a project that gets you noticed, or just start keeping track of your wins.

As an example, say your goal is to become your team's go-to for data visualization and present a dashboard project in the next all-hands:

- **Quarterly goal:** Be recognized as the data visualization resource and present at an all-hands.
- **Month 1:** Take an interactive Tableau course and make two dashboards using company data.
- **Month 2:** Help a peer with their report and request manager feedback.
- **Month 3:** Teach colleagues in a training session; present your dashboard to the team.

QUARTERLY CAREER ACTION PLAN

Quarterly Focus:			
SMART Goal (Specific, Measurable, Achievable, Relevant, Time-Bound)			
Month 1 Actions	**Month 2 Actions**	**Month 3 Actions**	**Metrics / Evidence**
• • •	• • •	• • •	• • •

Quarterly Review: Wins | Roadblocks | Adjustments		

Every step is something you can easily do, and together, they add up to real progress, not just wishful thinking.

Checking in on your progress is just as important as setting goals in the first place. You wouldn't wait until you're hopelessly lost to look at your GPS, right? At the end of each quarter, take an hour to look back: What did you get done? Where did things go off the rails? What needs a tweak? Don't beat yourself up; this is a chance to learn. Ask yourself: *What am I proud of this quarter? Which skills made a difference? Where did I get stuck, and what did I figure out? Did I leave anything half-finished? Do my goals still make sense for where I want to go?*

A simple reflection worksheet can help. Just split a page into three columns: "Wins," "Roadblocks," and "Next Steps." Jot down every win, no matter how tiny (finally nailed that presentation? Automated a boring task? It all counts). Under "Roadblocks," write what got in your way—maybe that online course was much harder than you thought, or a surprise project threw off your plans. In "Next Steps," figure out what you'll try differently next time, like blocking out more time to learn or asking for help sooner.

Sample Quarterly Review Prompts

- What accomplishment am I most proud of this quarter?
- Which new skill or habit made the biggest difference?
- Where did I hit resistance or setbacks, and what did I learn?
- Did I start but not finish something, and why?
- Are my original goals still relevant?

Be aware that plans almost never go exactly as you pictured. Maybe your promotion was put on ice because of a hiring freeze, or that course you signed up for turned out to be way over your head. That's just how it goes. The trick isn't to give up or spiral; it's to hit reset and reframe. Here's a quick checklist for adjusting your goals:

1. Pause and review: What changed?
2. Revisit priorities: What matters most now?
3. Adjust timelines or break big goals into smaller pieces.
4. Swap out goals that no longer fit for new ones.
5. Recognize and celebrate progress, even if it's different from what was planned.

For instance, say Carla aimed to lead a cross-functional project but was reassigned mid-quarter to a crisis team. At first, it felt like failure. But, after reviewing the experience, Carla recognized new skills, communication, collaboration, problem-solving, and positive attention from new leaders. Instead of "missed my milestone," Carla logged, "adapted quickly to change and built new relationships." She set her next goal to deepen those connections.

It's totally okay to change direction when life throws you a curveball. Progress always beats perfection.

To stay organized, use visual templates and digital tools that make tracking progress engaging and easy. If you're into digital solutions, Notion is great for custom dashboards, Trello works well for task cards (think "To Do," "In Progress," "Done," or "Stuck"), and Google Sheets is ideal for trend-tracking and color-coding your progress.

If you're more of a pen-and-paper person, print out a simple chart for the quarter (just boxes for goals, milestones, blockers, and wins) and stick it somewhere you'll see it. Crossing off each milestone as you go is weirdly satisfying, like giving yourself a gold star for adulting.

Interactive Element: Quarterly Review Dashboard

Set up a Quarterly Career Progress Dashboard using your tool of choice. Here's how:

1. Give your dashboard a title for the quarter's focus (e.g., "Summer 2026: Skill-Building & Visibility").
2. List SMART goals for the quarter.
3. Break down monthly milestones for each goal.
4. Track weekly actions (e.g., hours learning, meetings led).
5. Add sections for obstacles.
6. Celebrate every win: Throw in some emojis, stickers, or go wild with color-coding if that's your thing.
7. Calendar an end-of-quarter review session now.
8. At the review, reflect: What accomplishments make you proud? What could be tweaked? What surprised you?

Tweak your setup until it works for you. If something feels like a hassle, switch it up; no need to let your tracking tool turn into another thing you dread.

Research shows that structured progress-tracking increases achievement rates far more than scattered notes or vague intentions. Tools like Notion and Trello offer templates, and printable charts abound online if you prefer paper. The fanciest system isn't the best; the one that works for you is.

Remember: Don't think of this as busywork. You're making sure all your effort leads somewhere. When life inevitably throws you a curveball, these regular check-ins help you stay on track with what matters now, without losing sight of the big picture.

Momentum isn't about waiting for some huge break; it's about stacking up those small wins, one after another. Quarterly planning and honest check-ins are what move your career forward, even when everything feels up in the air.

Building Your Personal Advisory Board: Feedback, Mentorship, and Support

We have all faced big career questions: Should you accept that job offer, prep for a negotiation, or consider a pivot? Now picture having a group of wise, invested people in your corner who know your strengths and won't sugarcoat their advice. That's your personal advisory board. It's not just for CEOs; it's for anyone seeking clear answers, faster growth, and fewer regrets.

A personal advisory board is a carefully chosen group with diverse strengths and perspectives. Think of it as your career's team of superheroes (minus the spandex). You don't need many people; four to six is ideal, enough for varied input without overwhelming scheduling. The roles matter: a mentor whose path you admire, a sponsor who can advocate for you, a peer experiencing similar challenges, an industry expert tracking trends, and an accountability partner dedicated to follow-through. Each brings a unique viewpoint and support type. Mapping these out (mentor here, sponsor there, accountability buddy in the next bubble) turns your network into a strategic safety net.

To build your board, identify people for each role, not just those conveniently available. List those whose feedback helped you, those with admirable careers, or people who are always ahead of the curve. Don't stress if your ideal mentor is in another department, or your expert only knows you through LinkedIn; diversity matters. A board made entirely of people just like you creates an echo chamber.

When reaching out, be personal and specific. Nobody likes a vague "Can I pick your brain?" email. For a mentor, try: "I respect how you moved from analyst to team lead. Would you be open to a quarterly catch-up so I can learn from your experience?" For an expert: "You spot trends early in marketing. Would you share your take on this year's outlook?" Sponsors should already know your work firsthand and be willing to vouch for you. For peers: "I'm forming a small group to share progress and tackle challenges. Are you interested?" Most people are flattered to be asked for their insight, as long as it's clear why you chose them.

Your board doesn't need to come from one company, city, or even country. Your accountability partner might be in Berlin working night shifts, and your mentor could be a past boss in Toronto. Some do monthly coffee meetings; others keep it virtual with quarterly Zooms or rapid-fire group chats.

Once someone agrees, make it easy for them to support you. Set clear expectations. If you want quarterly check-ins or occasional updates, say so. Avoid ambiguous calendar invites with no agenda. Before meetings, send a quick note: "Here's what I'm working on, what I'm stuck on, and one thing I'd like your view on." This lets them prepare meaningful advice and avoid awkward silences.

Maintain relationships with simple, meaningful touchpoints. Every few weeks or months, send an update; no need for essays. A quick "Just did my first team presentation thanks to your slide-structuring advice!" goes a long way and makes people want to keep supporting you. Express gratitude at milestones, or when advice pays off. People remember these moments.

Set a cadence that works: For mentors or sponsors, monthly or quarterly meetings usually suffice unless you hit a crossroad. Peers or accountability partners might check in weekly or drop notes in a group chat. Industry experts only need to meet a couple of times a year, as long as it's relevant and appreciated.

Sample Templates

- **Progress update:** "Just landed my first client—your pricing advice worked!"
- **Gratitude:** "Thanks for reviewing my résumé. Your tips got me in the door."
- **General check-in:** "Exploring roles in data analytics, would love your perspective on trends."

Your board is vital when things get messy. Suppose you receive two job offers: one with great pay but a so-so culture, another with flexibility but less money. Instead of overthinking, consult your board. Your sponsor weighs long-term upsides, your expert flags future industry trends, your accountability partner asks practical questions, and your mentor helps align decisions with your values.

Brainstorming is another benefit. If you need to discuss workload with your boss, test scenarios with your board. They might suggest opening with curiosity or remind you to document your impact. Considering a career pivot? An industry expert can tell you about market realities, and a peer can offer encouragement.

Peer accountability groups boost momentum. Imagine four friends with weekly check-ins: each shares a win, a challenge, and a plan. You'll be more motivated, pick up their lessons, and learn faster by sharing failures and wins.

Reciprocity matters. Don't just ask for help. Offer value back. If someone's curious about AI, and you see a relevant article, forward it. Hear about an event they'd like to attend? Share details. Want to introduce two contacts? Always check with them first. These are about mutual, genuine support, not transactions.

Mapping these relationships visually, simple circles labeled "mentor," "sponsor," etc., with names, helps you spot gaps ("Too many from marketing. I need someone from outside the field!") and encourages a more balanced network.

A personal advisory board isn't about impressive names for LinkedIn, it's about honest feedback, fresh ideas, and trusted support for decisions big and small. Over time, these relationships make career growth less lonely, less random, and more rewarding.

Most people genuinely want to help if they understand what you need and know the relationship is two-way. That blend of generosity, structure, encouragement, and shared wins builds resilience for whatever challenges your career brings next.

Staying Future-Ready: Skill Refresh, Industry Trends, and Adaptability

Staying future-ready doesn't mean jumping on every new trend or becoming an instant expert in whatever's buzzing online. Instead, it means you're establishing straightforward habits to spot changes, update your skills regularly, and adapt to shifts in your field. You don't have to adopt every new tool; you just need a basic system that keeps you aware, without overwhelming you with information.

First, track what's happening in your industry. Don't depend on last-minute Slack chats or hearsay to stay updated, as that invites unnecessary stress. Instead, subscribe to a few targeted newsletters or blogs that filter industry news for you. For example, marketers might use "Marketing Brew" or "Content Marketing Institute," while those in tech could opt for "TL;DR" or "Stack Overflow Trends." This narrows your focus to the most relevant updates.

Expand your learning by following a couple of thought leaders on LinkedIn or X, choosing people who share clear, practical insights, not just industry noise. The size of their audience isn't important;

prioritize those who teach you something. Additionally, professional communities and forums (like Slack, Discord, Facebook groups, or Reddit) provide real, unfiltered discussion about what's really happening in day-to-day work.

Practical Tracking Tips

Create a "Trends" folder in your inbox or workspace for storing valuable newsletters or links. There's no pressure to read them immediately; just set aside 30 minutes each week to skim the highlights and note anything relevant. This keeps you informed without taking much time.

Keeping skills fresh is as crucial as trend-tracking. Many people find that their expertise quietly becomes outdated if they never intentionally update it. Avoid this with an annual "skills audit": Once a year, list your main skills and compare them to what's current in job ads and discussions in your field. Ask yourself: *Which skills do I use regularly? Which ones feel dated? What new tools or processes do I keep hearing about?*

Skill Refresh in Action

Once you've found your gaps, schedule regular learning. Rather than cramming, plan to take one class, workshop, or project each quarter. Online platforms like Coursera, LinkedIn Learning, and YouTube are great for this. The key isn't mastery, just steady progress. A few learning hours every month keep your skills sharp and marketable.

Ignore the illusion that everyone else is far ahead. Most people are just as uncertain about new tech, but they stay current by experimenting and asking questions early. Routine skill upgrades put you ahead of those who only act when it's absolutely necessary.

Adaptability: The Critical Mindset

Technical skill alone isn't enough if you're entrenched in old habits. Adaptability, being willing to learn and switch direction, is what ensures long-term career health. Periodically ask yourself, *What's changing in my field? How can I get ahead?* This guards against drifting into autopilot.

Consider Olivia, who worked in retail but noticed that online sales were rising. She learned e-commerce tools and helped launch website updates, so when remote work surged, she was ready for a logistics role others struggled to fill. Or Marcus, who pivoted from traditional health education to digital wellness after observing telehealth growth. Instead of waiting for his role to shrink, he enrolled in a short telehealth certification course, attended virtual healthcare technology webinars, and volunteered to help his organization pilot online workshops. He also revamped his materials for video delivery and learned the basics of remote patient engagement platforms. His proactive approach made him a leader, not a laggard.

Adaptability is more about regular curiosity than giant leaps. When something new appears, ask yourself: *Will this catch on? What's my first step to try it? Who can help me learn?* Even shadowing a colleague virtually for an hour can give you a practical edge.

Exploration Goals: Small Doses of Experimentation

To avoid stagnation, set quarterly "exploration goals," which aren't targets, just permission to try new things. Each quarter, pick one trend or tool outside your comfort zone and spend a few hours investigating. Try out an AI tool, attend a webinar on sustainability, or join a cross-team project.

Low-risk ways to explore include signing up for webinars (often free), joining micro-projects or hackathons, shadowing someone for a task, or sitting in on an info call with another team. If something catches your interest, dive deeper next quarter; if not, no big deal. This keeps your career flexible and prevents burnout, focusing on curiosity, not constant hustle.

Track your learning with a simple "exploration log" in Notion or Google Sheets. Quarterly, record what you tried, what you learned, and any new ideas sparked, even if it just confirmed something wasn't for you. Over time, you'll see what skills and trends you adapt to most easily.

Sustainable Progress

This system is built for real life: If you fall off for a quarter, just check your log and resume when ready. Progress comes from persistence, not perfection.

Staying future-ready means noticing what matters before it's urgent and making time to upgrade at your own pace. It also makes room for happy coincidences; the experiments you try can lead to unexpected opportunities.

Remember, future-ready professionals aren't born that way; they become future-ready by consistently paying attention and taking small risks before they're critical. Make habits that allow you to spot changes early, schedule regular skills refreshes, nurture adaptability, and allow for occasional exploration outside your job description.

These systems create momentum, keeping your career not just afloat, but moving ahead of the current. With these habits, you'll confidently meet whatever comes next, ready to act decisively instead of scrambling to react.

Taken together, these strategies help you make big career decisions with far more clarity and confidence. When opportunity, or chaos, arrives, you won't be scrambling. You'll be ready to respond thoughtfully and on your own terms.

Conclusion

Look at you, making it all the way to the end of this career rollercoaster. When you first cracked open this book, I'm guessing you were hoping for more than just a "work hard and hope for the best" pep talk. You wanted the real stuff: how to make smarter moves, negotiate without sweating through your shirt, and build a career that doesn't eat your weekends or your sanity for breakfast. That's what you just got: a step-by-step game plan for ambitious folks who want actual progress, not just another round of vague advice or a LinkedIn post that makes you roll your eyes.

Let's take a quick victory lap and see where you've been. You started by figuring out what matters to you: your values, your strengths, and the stuff you refuse to put up with (like answering emails at midnight or pretending "free stress" is a perk). You mapped out a career path that fits you, not some random idea of success you found online. You learned the difference between collecting skills like merit badges and picking the ones that make a difference. You waded into the world of communication, from giving and getting feedback that's helpful to managing up without turning into your boss's shadow and handling awkward conversations like a pro, or at least like someone who's practiced in the bathroom mirror a few times.

You took on salary negotiation and said goodbye to the days of just nodding and hoping for the best. Now you've got scripts, research tricks, and the guts to talk money and benefits like you're chatting about weekend plans. You found out that networking isn't about collecting business cards like Pokémon or pretending to be the loudest person in the room. It's about building real connections, even if your idea of a wild night is reading a book with a cup of tea instead of schmoozing at some networking event.

You figured out how to make smart pivots, size up job offers without spiraling into decision dread, and tell your story in a way that makes sense (to other people and to yourself). You built a personal brand that highlights your real strengths, rather than being just a pile of buzzwords. You learned to spot the secret codes of company culture and office politics, all without turning into "that guy" or losing your soul in the process. You saw that boundaries and resilience aren't just nice extras; they're the glue that keeps your career from falling apart. And you wrapped it all up with action plans, progress dashboards, and the reminder that growth involves small, regular steps, not some giant leap you make once a year.

Here's what really matters as you walk away from this book:

- **Self-clarity is your launchpad.** The more you know about your own drivers, the easier it is to make decisions that stick.
- **Skills and communication, not just effort, open doors.** People don't magically notice quiet, heads-down work. Show your value. Speak up.
- **Negotiation is a skill, not a secret club.** You can learn it. You can get better. And you deserve to.

- **Networking involves making real connections, not schmoozing.** Reach out. Help others. It pays off, sometimes in surprising ways.
- **Your personal brand is your story, not your slogan.** Be real, be specific, and let your work and reputation do some of the talking.
- **Workplace rules are often unwritten; learn to read between the lines.** Ask questions. Observe. Adjust without losing yourself.
- **Boundaries and resilience are non-negotiable.** Protect your energy like you protect your phone battery at 2%; no one else will do it for you.
- **Reflection and learning keep you moving.** Careers aren't puzzles you solve once. They're games you get better at every round.

You've put in the work by reading, thinking, scribbling notes in the margins, and maybe even rolling your eyes at my jokes (I get it). That's something to celebrate. You're not the same person you were when you started. Now you've got a toolkit that's ready to go.

If you're still feeling a bit skeptical, remember that every career path looks different, and sometimes progress moves at the speed of a sleepy snail. You'll hit setbacks (everyone does, even the people who look like they have it all together). Those moments aren't proof you're failing; they just mean you're in the game. The only real mistake is thinking you have to do it all alone or nail it on the first try.

So here's my challenge: Don't just close this book and let it collect dust (yes, even digital dust is a thing). Pick one thing, just one. Maybe it's updating your LinkedIn headline with something catchier, or setting up a feedback chat, or building your own dashboard, or even writing a negotiation email you don't send yet. Whatever it is, do it this week. Momentum isn't magic; it's just habit in disguise.

And don't stop there. Come back to the frameworks, scripts, and checklists whenever you hit a crossroads or run face-first into a wall. Your career will keep changing, and that's a good thing. Treat this whole process like a living, breathing experiment. Check your dashboard. Celebrate your wins. Tweak your goals. Repeat. The best careers aren't built in a straight line; they zig, they zag, and sometimes they do a full loop-de-loop. That's not chaos; that's just how progress looks in real life.

I hope you remember you're not supposed to do this solo. Accountability buddies, mentors, and peer groups can make all the difference. Share your goals, ask for feedback, and help others out, too. Growth is a team sport, even if you'd rather be on the bench with a book.

Thanks for letting me tag along on your journey. I wrote this book because I believe in people like you, folks who want more than empty hustle or advice that sounds like it was written by a robot. I believe you can negotiate with confidence, stand up for yourself, and grow without burning out or second-guessing every move. You've got the tools, the frameworks, and most importantly, the self-awareness to steer your own course.

Your next chapter is waiting. Step into it with intention, resilience, and a good helping of self-compassion. Build a career that fits your life, not the other way around. Stay curious, stay bold, and remember: Forward is forward, even if you're moving at turtle speed.

Now, go make your next move. I'll be over here, cheering you on from the sidelines.

References

- CareerFoundry. (2025). *The 13 best online learning platforms in 2025.* https://careerfoundry.com/en/blog/career-change/best-online-learning-platforms/
- Castrillon, C. (2025, March). *The hidden truths of corporate life: 5 myths debunked.* Forbes. https://www.forbes.com/sites/carolinecastrillon/2025/03/11/the-hidden-truths-of-corporate-life-5-myths-debunked/
- Castrillon, C. (2025, April). *How to navigate office politics without selling your soul.* Forbes. https://www.forbes.com/sites/carolinecastrillon/2025/04/09/how-to-navigate-office-politics-without-selling-your-soul/
- ContactMonkey. (2024, September). *How to implement effective employee feedback loops.* https://www.contactmonkey.com/blog/employee-feedback-loops
- Corporate Job Bank. (2025, January). *The rise of portfolio careers: Navigating multiple roles in the modern workforce.* https://corporatejobbank.com/the-rise-of-portfolio-careers-navigating-multiple-roles-in-the-modern-workforce/
- DiversityJobs. (2023). *How to turn diversity into a career advantage.* https://www.diversityjobs.com/career-advice/career-advice/how-to-turn-diversity-into-a-career-advantage/
- Engagedly. (2025, June). *Mastering the SBI feedback model: Definition and examples.* https://engagedly.com/blog/importance-of-sbi-when-giving-feedback-in-workplace/
- FlexJobs. (n.d.). *Portfolio career: Definition, pros & cons, and getting started.* https://www.flexjobs.com/blog/post/how-to-have-a-portfolio-career
- Harvard Business Review. (2021, August). *Everything you need to know about stock options and RSUs.* https://hbr.org/2021/08/everything-you-need-to-know-about-stock-options-and-rsus
- Harvard Business Review. (2022, April). *A guide to setting better boundaries.* https://hbr.org/2022/04/a-guide-to-setting-better-boundaries
- Harvard Business Review. (2025). *Soft skills matter now more than ever, according to new research.* https://hbr.org/2025/08/soft-skills-matter-now-more-than-ever-according-to-new-research
- Harvard Extension School. (2019, April). *Future-proof job skills: What employees need to know.* https://extension.harvard.edu/blog/future-proof-job-skills-what-employees-need-to-know/
- Hive. (2023, April). *How to turn down extra work politely: 9 phrases & examples.* https://hive.com/blog/how-to-turn-down-extra-work-politely/

- Indeed Editorial Team. (2025). *7 steps you can take to use a decision matrix template.* https://www.indeed.com/career-advice/career-development/decision-matrix-template
- Indeed Editorial Team. (2025). *How to make a digital portfolio in 5 steps (plus tips).* https://www.indeed.com/career-advice/finding-a-job/how-to-make-digital-portfolio
- Indeed Editorial Team. (2025). *Personal brand statement examples (with steps and tips).* https://ca.indeed.com/career-advice/career-development/personal-brand-statement-examples
- Indeed Editorial Team. (2025). *Salary negotiation scripts to counter any job offer.* https://www.indeed.com/career-advice/pay-salary/salary-negotiation-script
- Indeed Editorial Team. (2025). *What are T-shaped skills? (And why they are important).* https://www.indeed.com/career-advice/resumes-cover-letters/t-shaped-skills
- InvestGlass. (2025). *12 best tools for setting and tracking goals.* https://www.investglass.com/pl/12-best-tools-for-setting-and-tracking-goals-complete-guide-for-2025/
- LinkedIn. (n.d.). *How to research salary benchmarks before a review.* https://www.linkedin.com/top-content/negotiation/preparing-for-a-salary-review-negotiation/how-to-research-salary-benchmarks-before-a-review/
- LinkedIn. (n.d.). *LinkedIn strategies for early career professionals.* https://www.linkedin.com/top-content/networking/linkedin-professional-guidelines/linkedin-strategies-for-early-career-professionals/
- LinkedIn Talent Solutions. (2024, February). *The most in-demand skills of 2024.* https://www.linkedin.com/business/talent/blog/talent-strategy/linkedin-most-in-demand-hard-and-soft-skills
- Liu, J. (2023, May). *How to craft a LinkedIn profile that recruiters love.* Forbes. https://www.forbes.com/sites/josephliu/2023/05/22/the-ultimate-guide-to-crafting-a-linkedin-profile-that-recruiters-love-advice-from-100-hiring-professionals/
- Mayo Clinic Staff. (2023, November). *Job burnout: How to spot it and take action.* https://www.mayoclinic.org/healthy-lifestyle/adult-health/in-depth/burnout/art-20046642
- OpenNews. (2021, September). *Network mapping: Learn a 30-minute strategy to find the right connections.* https://source.opennews.org/articles/network-mapping-learn-30-minute-strategy/
- Perlow, L. A. (2012). *Sleeping with your smartphone: How to break the 24/7 habit and change the way you work.* Harvard Business Review Press. https://www.hbs.edu/faculty/Pages/item.aspx?num=42507
- Psychiatry.org. (2025, February). *Preventing burnout: A guide to protecting your well-being.* https://www.psychiatry.org/news-room/apa-blogs/preventing-burnout-protecting-your-well-being

- ReputationDefender. (2023, June). *The ultimate career hack for your college grad*. Medium. https://reputationdefender.medium.com/the-ultimate-career-hack-for-your-college-grad-secrets-from-reputation-management-experts-c64bf6847b62
- Robert Half. (2024, May). *5 strategies for remote workers to grow a visible, vibrant career*. https://www.roberthalf.com/us/en/insights/research/6-strategies-for-remote-workers-to-grow-a-visible-vibrant-career
- Shorthand. (n.d.). *10 best (and free!) tools to create your online portfolio*. https://shorthand.com/the-craft/online-portfolio-tools/indcx.html
- SmartBrief. (2025, October). *The job seeker's guide to reading company culture*. https://www.smartbrief.com/original/the-job-seekers-guide-to-reading-company-culture
- Smartsheet. (2025, September). *Free goal setting and tracking templates*. https://www.smartsheet.com/goal-tracking-setting-templates
- Southern Methodist College. (n.d.). *Sample informational interview script*. https://www.smc.edu/student-support/career-services/explore-majors-and-careers/informational-interviewing/sample-informational-interview-scripts.php
- TechTarget. (2024, March). *5 remote work communication challenges and how to fix them*. https://www.techtarget.com/searchunifiedcommunications/tip/Remote-work-communication-challenges-and-how-to-fix-them
- TripleTen. (2025). *Career plateau? 7 signs you're stuck and how to break free*. https://tripleten.com/blog/posts/career-plateau-7-clear-signs-youre-stuck--and-how-to-break-free
- University of Texas at San Antonio. (n.d.). *Assembling your personal board of advisors* (PDF). https://provost.utsa.edu/mentoring/docs/personal-board-advisors.pdf

KEEP GROWING WITH THE BLUEPRINT SERIES

If you found this helpful, continue building real-world confidence with these practical guides for teens and young adults.

Money Skills for Teens Blueprint

by Noah Clark

Build a strong foundation in budgeting, saving, credit, and smart money habits.

Perfect for teens who want confidence before adulthood hits.

Practical Life Skills for Young Adults

by Noah Clark

Develop practical skills in cooking, home maintenance, organization, and everyday adulting.

Everything school forgot to teach.

Financial Literacy for Young Adults Blueprint

by Noah Clark

Take control of investing, student loans, debt, long-term planning, and financial independence.

Money decisions made simple.

No overwhelm. No jargon. Just practical skills that actually matter.